UNMASKED

Two Confidential Interviews with Hitler in
1931

by

EDOUARD CALIC

With a Foreword by
Professor Golo Mann

Translated from the German by
RICHARD BARRY

1971
CHATTO & WINDUS
LONDON

Published by
Chatto & Windus Ltd
40 William IV Street
London, W.C.2

*

Clarke, Irwin & Co. Ltd
Toronto

ISBN 0 7011 1642 0

First published in German under the title
Ohne Maske

© Frankfurter Societäts-Druckerei GmbH 1968

English translation © Chatto & Windus Ltd 1971

Printed in Great Britain by
Northumberland Press Ltd
Gateshead

CONTENTS

FOREWORD

Innumerable authentic Hitler documents of the 1933-1945 period are available – shorthand records of speeches to private audiences or of 'briefing conferences', minutes of negotiations or interviews, memoirs both from Germans and foreigners whose duties brought them in contact with the dictator. For the period before the seizure of power, however, material is sparse – and yet this is the phase of the greatest interest to Hitler's biographers. Here the politician is seen developing; he is not yet the fully-fledged schemer employing and repeating his wiles until at last – at last – the world at large could see through them and react in the right way. This period shows the astounding continuity of Hitler's thoughts and intentions. He was a remarkably evil and repellent being – a monster. One thing, however, he had in common with other great figures of history: very early on he foresaw, in fact he knew, what he wanted, what he had in him, what would one day happen around him and become reality. The French statesman's remark: *on est Premier Ministre pour l'avoir voulu*, is entirely applicable to Hitler. He became the 'Führer', the tyrant, the conqueror, he gave Germany hegemony over Eurasia, perhaps not for a thousand years but at least for two or three, all because he wanted it that way. Basically that was all there was to it. There is not much competition in the struggle for power, far less than in business. A lot of people want to become rich. But who really wants power, total power?

Let us not oversimplify. There was more to it than that in Hitler's case – a highly developed intuitive, though disordered, brain, talent for organisation and delegation

7

without loss of control, imagination, cunning, knowledge of and disdain for men; he also possessed the capacity, so necessary in his 'profession', of differentiating between essentials and non-essentials. He can, unfortunately must, therefore, be classified as a 'great man' – always provided that 'greatness' has nothing to do with morality and that it can be combined with insanity.

From his knowledge of men came the art of handling them. Hitler invariably adapted himself to anyone he was talking to. That does not mean that he was a deliberate liar (though he did lie). Not only did he say what seemed most advantageous to say at the time; he actually believed it. Such liars are always the most convincing.

I have always thought that the most instructive pre-1933 Hitler conversations were those published by Hermann Rauschning in 1939. Rauschning was President of the Danzig Senate and a National-Socialist himself; Hitler gave him real insight into his mind. This is why the 'next war', how it was to be fought and for what purposes, is so often referred to in these talks. People have been at pains to prove that Hitler 'did not want' the Second World War – A. J. P. Taylor, for instance, has made this mistake. As if that was the point. He wanted war; war was in his bones from the outset. But war when it happens always looks somewhat different from war *per se*, from war in the abstract.

In the conversations recorded in this book Hitler refers to war hardly at all. There was good reason for that. Breiting, to whom he was talking, was not a convinced supporter and in fact had many reservations; he was a conservative, a solid German citizen. He felt both attracted and repelled by the National-Socialist leader. Attracted because Hitler was a 'constructive force' (as the term then was), a nationalist, a sworn enemy of communism, a despiser of social democracy, an abhorrer of the 'shameful Versailles diktat'. All these views Breiting inevitably found satisfactory. But he was repelled because the spell-binder was, after all, rather too radical. Anti-semitism – well and good, but surely there were some decent people among the Jews. Anti-communism – first-class, but what did Hitler think about the sanctity of private property? Of course the contemporary Reichstag was useless, but would it not be dangerous to rule without parliament altogether? This was what the prosperous Saxon bourgeois thought. Yet while waiting to be ushered in, he could not help admiring the forbidding splendour of the 'Brown House' and the smooth-running Party machine.

Hitler realised at once what sort of a person his visitor was. He played the honest man. In fact he was honest; it is not necessary to say everything one thinks in order to be honest. He used his skill, the only skill he shared with Bismarck, of bemusing people by telling them the truth. In *Mein Kampf* he had not concealed his scorn for 'the people', the German people included; similarly he did not conceal from Breiting his scorn for the German bourgeoisie. They were thoroughly corrupt and opportunist, he said; they would come along as soon as he brandished the whip; he would need them, the industrialists, the bankers and the professors, but he would never allow himself to be ruled by them. And so it turned out. He forecast the developments of the next few years with astonishing acumen: the alliance with the German Nationalists, the seizure of power through a democratic parliamentary majority, the destruction of the parliamentary system immediately thereafter. But because he wished to win Breiting over, he was careful not to tell him all. He had no intention of massacring the Jews – perhaps at the time he really had not. Jew-murder was in him, but not yet as a conscious determination – that only emerged as a result of the war situation. He presented himself as a protagonist of strict order – which he was; he did not, however, present himself as a creator of chaos, which he also was and in a far truer sense. He did not tell Breiting, as he did Rauschning, that if necessary he would carry the world with him into the abyss; he did not play the funeral motif from *Götterdämmerung*. And so he achieved what he wanted by an inimitable mixture of brutal honesty and the art of concealment. Breiting went away highly impressed. He had never met a politician like this before. This was the coming man.

Anyone who knows Hitler from other documents will recognise him again here and will learn something more about this most grisly human phenomenon of a century rich in grisly events.

Kilchberg am Zürichsee   GOLO MANN
16 March 1968

INTRODUCTION

In two confidential interviews, given in May and June 1931, Adolf Hitler, the leader of the National-Socialist German Workers Party, explained his aims and his plans to Richard Breiting,[1] editor of the *Leipziger Neueste Nachrichten*. Having assured himself that his statements would be kept secret, Hitler analysed the situation and unfolded a programme for action and plans for the future which could not have been deduced either from his speeches or from his book *Mein Kampf* or from the Nazi Party's programme. He spoke of the role to be played in his strategy for the 'legal' seizure of power by the bourgeoisie, industry, the military, the church and the 'plastic' mass of the people; he painted a picture of his future authoritarian tyranny and of the planned transformation of all aspects of public life from the law to the press. In the second interview he dealt with his plans for the transformation of Europe once the Soviet Union had been destroyed, moving about European states from Scandinavia to the Mediterranean, from France to the Balkans, like chessmen. He rubbed some states off the map and prophesied a great migration eastwards. He allotted England, the USA and the colonial empires their future role and ended with a world dominated by the white nordic race.

How did it come about that in 1931 Hitler revealed his wishes and his plans so frankly and comprehensively to a representative of the press?

The *Leipziger Neueste Nachrichten* was a great German daily newspaper, founded in 1892, edited and published by 'Edgar Herfurth and Co.'; it represented the policy of the conservative Right, the German National Peoples Party and the right wing of the German Peoples Party.[2] It supported the

11

political aims of the men around Hugenberg. Breiting, the editor, was on terms of confidence with Oberfohren, floor-leader of the German Nationals. Being nationalist minded and intent on information, the paper rated the NSDAP as a 'political reality'; it had opposed the speaking ban on Hitler and the disbandment of his paramilitary formations; it had several times spoken out for his naturalisation.

In 1930, when Hitler captured 6·4 million votes in the Reichstag elections, he founded a newspaper in Dresden for the 'Saxony Gau'; it was called the *Freiheitskampf*. It could not, however, compete with the well-established and well-directed *Leipziger Neueste Nachrichten*. The *Freiheitskampf*'s reader public was small and not to be taken seriously. Conservative readers found it vulgar and elementary since it tried to make its way by scandal- and sensation-mongering. It vilified Herfurth and Breiting as amoral and corrupt; it maintained that, under cover of the nationalist opposition they were trying to perpetuate the 'boss policy of the present system'. In 1931 these attacks reached such heights that Herfurth and Breiting were forced to complain to Hitler.

Breiting had no difficulty in gaining entrée to the leader of the NSDAP. From 1928 to 1930 Dr. Otto Dietrich had been his Munich correspondent and had proved a reliable source of information on everything to do with the Nazi Party, giving Herfurth and Breiting useful 'confidential reports' on Hitler's policy. Breiting and Dietrich were on friendly terms and these continued when Dietrich left the paper and transferred to the *Essener Nationalzeitung*, the Nazi Gau newspaper founded in 1930 with financial support from certain industrialists with Göring as intermediary. Dietrich married the daughter of Dr. Reismann-Grone, the publisher, who owned the *Rheinische-Westfälische Zeitung*, also backed by heavy industry. As son-in-law to an influential publisher Dietrich could be most useful to the NSDAP and keep Hitler informed on the tendencies in industrial

12

circles. At the same time he used his position to 'interpret' Hitler's economic policy and anti-semitic views. Hitler made good use of Dietrich's contacts and at the same time castigated the publishers in order the better to be able to blackmail them. In 1931 he made Dietrich Press Chief of the NSDAP and in 1937 rewarded him with the title of Reich Press Chief. Via Otto Dietrich Breiting was granted an interview with Hitler in Munich in May 1931.

When Hitler decided that the time had come to assault the bourgeois press fortress, he already had a strong organisation and a number of newspapers which were feared rather than respected. Many people, intimidated by the Gau papers and their attacks, were persuaded to fill the Nazi Party coffers. Hitler had perceived that the major newspapers acted as efficient links between industry, finance, the Wehrmacht, the Herrenklub, the intellectuals, the senior State authorities and the bourgeois section of the electorate. At this stage of his struggle it was important to him to harness these circles to his purposes. Tactically he preferred to make temporary allies of his opponents. He therefore set out to obtain the goodwill of influential key figures among the conservatives by talking of the 'legality' of his road to power. Demagogic speeches were of no use here; he could only convince by explaining his tactics, the precision of his calculations and insisting on the inevitability of historical developments. He wished to turn accomplices into conspirators. This can be the only explanation for the fact that, under ban of secrecy, he revealed matters which might have been dangerous to him had they become public knowledge.

When Hitler received Breiting in Munich he was well informed about his visitor. He mentioned the recommendation from his information service. Undoubtedly he also knew what the Social-Democrat *Leipziger Volkszeitung* had said: 'Breiting, the editor-in-chief of the Herfurth newspaper has more say in the running of the paper than Edgar Herfurth himself; he rules "his" editors with a rod of iron; he is the unknown dictator, the all-powerful ruler of Leipzig's bourgeois parties'. The paper continued that Breiting was the man who gave Rothe, the Burgomaster of Leipzig, Blüher, the Burgomaster of Dresden, and Wilhelm Bünger, the ex-Minister-President of Saxony, their marching orders. 'Herr Breiting acts. Despite everything Bünger curries favour with him because he is afraid of the *Leipziger Neueste Nachrichten*.'

In these two interviews Hitler was trying to win over this 'real dictator' of public opinion. He expected Breiting to bring the *Leipziger Neueste Nachrichten* into line behind him and give effective support to his policy. Hitler was so forthcoming to Breiting that he permitted him to take shorthand notes, though he swore him and his companion, Dr. Alfred Detig, to secrecy.[3]

At the first interview, which took place on 4 May 1931 in the so-called 'Brown House' in Munich, Rudolf Hess, Hitler's secretary, was present. For the second interview early in June Breiting was unaccompanied. For part of the time Dr. Hans Frank, Hitler's legal adviser, was present since he was dealing with the dispute with the *Freiheitskampf*.[4]

These two conversations have remained unknown until now. Not until nearly three years later did Party headquarters remember that Breiting had taken notes. As the result of an indiscretion it became known that he had made a summary for Edgar Herfurth. Max Amann, the head of the Party publishing firm, and Goebbels, the Reich propaganda leader, also came to know of the interviews from Hitler's engagement list. As a result, on 18 February 1934 the Leipzig Gestapo demanded the return of all Breiting's notes on the grounds that they dealt with Hitler's thinking and that, should they become known, statements by the Führer before the seizure of power might be misinterpreted abroad. Breiting stated categorically that he had no papers and had destroyed his notes.

When the Nazis came to power Breiting tried to join the

Party in order to protect himself and his friends from persecution. Documentary evidence exists that the Leipzig Gestapo initiated secret proceedings against Breiting, accusing him of being a 'Jewish lackey' because he went about with Jews, did not use a National-Socialist lawyer for his affairs and accepted advertisements from Jewish firms in his paper. He was also accused of having 'deceived the highest authorities in an unworthy manner and given preferential treatment to Jews even before the seizure of power'. He was therefore refused admittance to the Party and threatened with legal proceedings for corruption and peculation.

Threatening Jews or those friendly to Jews with criminal proceedings or actually bringing them to court were typical methods employed by the Nazis after the seizure of power.

Before the purge of 30 June 1934 Breiting, who was suspect because of his connections with Bünger, the President of the Criminal Court which had conducted the Leipzig Trial, was accused of having divulged secrets about the Reichstag Fire to his friends in Berlin and even of spreading stories abroad. He could not, of course, be implicated in the Röhm *putsch*, since no one would have believed that tale. Seeing that he was interrogated several times between February and June 1934, however, it became known that the Gestapo and the Party in Leipzig had something against him in connection with the Reichstag Fire. Breiting was a close friend of Goerdeler, the Burgomaster, who was able to protect him.

On 19 April 1937 Breiting was summoned to the Reich Ministry of Propaganda in Berlin, where two Gestapo agents took him to a restaurant for a talk. Although he was only 54 and had hitherto been in good health, he returned to Leipzig racked with convulsions and a nervous fever. According to his family he was convinced that he had been poisoned. A week later he was dead. Though the family requested an autopsy, the doctor in charge refused. His body was cremated without his family's knowledge.

UNMASKED

In 1934 Richard Breiting hid all his personal documents, including the shorthand notes, with his sister Ella Breiting in Pinneberg near Hamburg. After 1945 his widow took over all his papers. The authenticity of the documents has been confirmed by sworn statements by his widow and by his grandson, Ekkehard Schneider-Breiting, a statement by Frau Tränkner, his ex-secretary, who transcribed the short-hand, a memorandum from Ludwig Krieger, a retired civil servant and ex-head of the Reichstag stenographic bureau, and the opinions of many eminent historians and experts on the Nazi period such as Karl Dietrich Bracher, Harold C. Deutsch, Emil Dovifat, Sebastian Haffner, Walther Hofer, Robert M. W. Kempner, Eugen Kogon, Karl Lange, Wolfgang Malanowski, Golo Mann, Wilhelm Ritter von Schramm, Henry Ashby Turner Jr., Friedrich Zipfel and others.

In his memorandum dated 8 September 1968 Krieger says: 'The transcript checks with the original ... Having been a shorthand writer at Hitler's briefing conferences in his headquarters during the Second World War, I recognise Hitler's style and reactions throughout the record. Breiting's papers as a whole confirm the sequence of events. Both from the factual and political points of view the checking of these papers has been of extreme interest to me. Breiting's shorthand record is assuredly of great historical value since, as far as I know, no shorthand notes of private discussions with Hitler in the pre-1933 period exist.'

These documents shed a new light on the history of the years 1931-1933. Within the limited scope of this book it has been impossible to analyse all the subjects which Hitler raised in his talks with Breiting. I have therefore confined myself to those of major importance for any interpretation of Hitler's ideology and tactics before his seizure of power.

EDOUARD CALIC

TRANSCRIPT
of Richard Breiting's Shorthand Notes

First Interview with Hitler, 4 May 1931

Hitler's headquarters is in the Brienner Strasse, Munich, in the ex-'Barlow Palace' where the Italian Legation was housed until the 1890s. Immediately opposite is the palace of the Papal Nuncio. The Brienner Strasse is one of the smartest streets in Munich. Hitler paid 500,000 marks for the Barlow Palace and spent as much again on alterations. The swastika flag flying from the roof can be seen a long way off. There are sentries on the door who check the papers of everyone entering; they give an impression of extremely strict martial discipline. All of them are fine large military figures, hard-faced, and one can well imagine them giving their lives for their movement.

Dr. Alfred Detig[1] and I were received at the door by Rudolf Hess, Hitler's private secretary and one of his oldest comrades-in-arms. Hess had taken part in the 1923 Feldherrnhalle *putsch*; a glance at him showed that he was an ex-officer; traces of mental turmoil showed in his face and undoubtedly he had a streak of fanaticism. Hess led us into the marble entrance hall. A plaque bore the names of the thirteen National-Socialists who fell in front of the Feldherrnhalle; one wall was lined with standards and Hess explained that the other was reserved for a memorial which would carry the names of the three hundred National-Socialists murdered or fallen in the cause of the Movement. The whole hall gave an impression of great solemnity and gravity. Swastika signs were everywhere, carved into the stucco ceiling, and even introduced into the valuable glass of the windows.

Since Hitler was not yet there, Hess took us on a tour of the place. Innumerable offices occupied the ground floor and the basement. Everything was brand-new and showed first-class organisation. We were taken into the records office in the basement lined with fire- and burglar-proof steel cupboards containing the personal files of the 500,000 members of the NSDAP. The records were designed to deal with a million names and Hess explained to us that, when the NSDAP had a million members, they would accept no more 'Either we can do it with a million or we can't do it at all.' Anyone applying for membership was only accepted after a year's probation. Members who did not pay were 'fired' at once.

Hitler's study and the offices of his immediate staff were on the first floor. The offices were fitted out in really exquisite artistic taste; everything was in genuine oak with valuable antique cupboards; some of the lights were chandeliers of old Venetian glass.

Hess took us into the 'Hall of Senators', a large, ornate, artistically furnished room containing 61 red leather chairs. The marble ceiling included a Party badge in mosaic; the floor was covered by vast priceless carpets into which were woven innumerable swastikas; on the wall facing the door, surmounted by an enormous swastika, were four plaques showing the phases in the NSDAP's development: formation, programme, initial setback and 'renewal' (on 14 September 1930).

The 'Hall of Senators', Hess explained, was intended later to seat the highest dignitaries of the NSDAP, the men qualified to rule Germany. Also of interest was a courtroom on the floor above, where the NSDAP supreme court sits. It made a dignified impression; the 'Court President's' chair stood in front of a semi-circular table; before him was a golden swastika and above a large figure of Christ.[2]

Our astonishment grew as we toured the great building. This palace, furnished with antiques and in exquisite artistic taste, was in glaring contrast to the offices of a 'workers' party'. One had the impression that Hitler lived here in royal state and that he really believed that this setting was his due as the future overlord of Germany.[3]

We had to wait a whole hour before we were received by Hitler. He has constant visitors. Hess told us that he works at extreme pressure from early morning till late at night. Visitors, he said, were mostly German and foreign politicians; the rumour that Hitler was shy and avoided interviews was untrue. The only people he would not receive were journalists since his experience of them so far had been bad. We were a laudable exception.

* * *

Hitler was sitting at a vast ambassadorial desk in a large study next to the 'Hall of Senators'; a picture of Mussolini stood on the desk; on the wall was an enormous oil painting of Frederick the Great.[4] Hess introduced us. I assured Hitler that I had not come to ask for an interview; I happened to have business in Munich and wished to make his acquaintance. Anyone active in public life 'could not, after all, disregard a personality such as Hitler'. This clearly oiled the wheels with Hitler, who had so far worn a stern impenetrable expression. He seemed highly honoured when I told him that Herr Edgar Herfurth, our editor, wished to devote a whole page to the leader of the NSDAP. Hitler shook my hand and said in a friendly, almost genial voice: 'I am pleased to meet you; I know the part which you and your paper play among the German intelligentsia and bourgeoisie.'

* * *

HITLER: 'Our information service has informed me of the position which you have adopted towards the great problems of today. I would therefore like to express my thanks to you. I think, however, that with men who have the courage to say how disgracefully the rights of the National-Socialist Movement are being trampled on, I should speak openly and not give a formal press interview ...'

(With a friendly gesture Hitler asks us to be seated. We sit down and he continues)

'It is doubtful whether you could publish my statements in the way I would wish. I know that they would be cut and continuity sentences inserted. I realise that. Like other newspapers, the *Leipziger Neueste Nachrichten* lives on advertisements. I would not want you to be boycotted in this respect by my enemies and the enemies of the nation. I do not ask you to devote a whole page to me and my statements. Both the Jews and a large part of the bourgeoisie with whom you have links, would declare an advertisement boycott against you. At this point it is far more important to me to speak openly with people who have the future of Germany at heart; I am less interested in what the Jews, the Vatican or the Communist International say. I therefore have no need for an interview and I have not received you for that purpose. For the NSDAP it is far more important that your paper should adopt a sensible attitude to those forces which are fighting indefatigably for the rebirth of Germany. You must therefore believe that it is essential to adopt an unequivocal attitude to National-Socialism and the rebirth of Germany. And this applies, not to you alone, but also to the proprietor of your newspaper, Herr Herfurth, and to the circles from which you draw your support. At this moment I have no need of newspapers; I need German men; I need you as a representative of our intelligentsia. I will speak openly with you; this house shall have no secrets for you. To avoid intrigue, I require from you a promise that what we discuss here will remain a matter between us and that no word of it be published. All must remain a matter between us.'[5]

BREITING: 'I give you my word and also that of my colleague, Dr. Detig.'

(Hitler makes no objection to my taking notes for my personal use. He knows that I was once a shorthand writer in the Reichstag)

HITLER (confidentially): 'The day is not far off when we shall be living in great times once more. What we now need is that intelligent writers should make clear to the citizens of Germany the historic turning point at which Germany stands today. We are on the threshold of a unique new epoch in our history. We have reached the turning point when the bourgeoisie must decide whether it will choose bolshevist chaos in Germany and therefore in Europe or a National-Socialist Germany and a new order on our continent. If they are to make this decision, certain ideas about our social structure and our fateful struggle must be made clear to the bourgeoisie, the intelligentsia and the army....'[6]

(Hitler looks contemplatively at the ceiling and continues)

'You are a representative of the bourgeoisie against which we are fighting. The bourgeoisie is to blame for its failure to weld into the nation the growing fourth estate, the industrialised proletariat. The bourgeoisie should have assumed leadership of this fourth estate instead of spurning it in their false arrogance and so enabling a man like Karl Marx with his internationalist doctrine to gain a foothold in the German working class. The nation has been split by the advent of Marx. On the right is the nationally-minded bourgeoisie whose thinking on social matters, however, is totally inadequate; on the left is the working class with its justified social demands but which, unfortunately, has become completely divorced from any thought of the nation through the influence of Marx. It is the business of the NSDAP to create a common platform upon which those now incited to revolt can find their place. This platform is called National-Socialism.'

BREITING: 'I am aware of these ideas, Herr Hitler, and I do not believe that you will be able to complete your task without the German bourgeoisie.'

(My remark took him by surprise; he suddenly changed his tone and replied curtly:)

HITLER: 'I do not need the bourgeoisie; the bourgeoisie needs me and my movement. I have brought the concept of National-Socialism into the world and I shall carry through its ideas brutally and, if necessary, by force. In this I feel myself the emissary of Fate, the standard bearer as I am sometimes called, and with my Movement I shall thump the drum until Germany wakes up. The NSDAP has one advantage over the bourgeoisie: the totality of its ideology. Over the last forty years the German bourgeoisie has been a lamentable failure; it has not given the German people a single leader;[7] it will have to bow without gainsaying to the totality of my ideology. I shall make no concessions. I have no need of a bank account in Switzerland or a villa in Travemünde or on the Bavarian lakes.[8] The bourgeoisie rules by intrigue, but it can have no foothold in my movement because we accept no Jews or Jewish accomplices into our Party. The bourgeoisie shows what it is capable of by the intrigues which it instigates against the Reichswehr, attempting to place a barrier between me and the officer corps. They call me a stateless corporal and a housepainter. Is there anything improper in having volunteered for the army and served as a corporal? Is there anything improper in having earned one's daily bread by manual labour? Even the Social Democrats, who call themselves a workers' party, use the same language when they want to insult me.[9] The day of reckoning is not far off. An increasing number of industrialists, financiers, intellectuals and officers are now looking for a man who will at last bring some order into affairs at home, who will draw the farmers, the workers and the officials into the German community once more. The crisis has not yet reached its peak. Unemployment cannot be dealt with by weekly contributions and soup kitchens. Unemployment and the economic crisis are grist to the communist mill.

The Bolshevik Trotsky calls upon the Socialists and Communists to make common cause against National-Socialism. High finance must recognise that, with a common marxist front, the economic crisis cannot be overcome. Yet there are financiers trying to torpedo our National-Socialist movement by bribery. They send petitions to Hindenburg and vilify us as provocateurs. Our mere appearance on the streets is a challenge to law and order, they say. Yet we are the ones who are fighting for order, for a solution to the crisis and the avoidance of anarchy.[10] No man shall stop us going on to the streets again. We wish to recapture the Germans – all of them. The primary aim of our policy is the resurrection of a young healthy nation. And if we demand that Germans do their duty for Germany, that is not provocative. If the masses can be set on the move, there can be no provocation. Are we to allow ourselves to be beaten by these parasites? Because they keep on saying that we are not to go on to the streets or hold meetings? Anyone who believes in the future of Germany knows that the traitors to the country can only be dealt with by direct fighting in the open. We shall continue to march and to stir up the masses until the last German has been recaptured for the national cause.[11] To show you what these Social Democrat parasites are capable of – last year General Groener, as Reichswehr Minister, allowed Lieutenant Wendt and 2nd Lieutenants Scheringer and Ludin to be arrested. Fortunately we have still got some honest senior officers like Colonel Beck,[12] who would never allow his profession to be betrayed. A General like Rundstedt would simply have had those policemen shot when they came to arrest Reichswehr officers. Groener, Schleicher[13] and the rest go on with their plotting but, when the decisive moment comes, the majority of officers will side with the political forces striving for the renewal of Germany.'

BREITING: 'Many of your supporters have emphasised that there is no question of a military *coup*. They are supposed to have said that 8 November 1923 was a *faux pas* and that you are determined to come to power solely by legal methods.'

HITLER (angrily): 'I have never said that our march to the Feldherrnhalle was a *faux pas*. At the time it was the only form of protest we could make and, as you see, we did not lose the people's confidence as a result; on the contrary, it has grown all the time. I do not for a moment conceive of coming to power with the help of the Generals or by means of a *putsch*. That does not mean, however, that we intend to be passive onlookers while our friends are accused, arrested and murdered. On our list of martyrs there are already the names of 300 men struck down by the communists or their minions.[14] Messrs von Papen and Hugenberg, von Hindenburg and von Rundstedt must, for once, guarantee law and order in the Reich or they will be swept away by the national flood. The terrorist groups and their patrons, now sitting in the highest seats in the Reich and the *Länder*, must have their teeth drawn. We shall welcome any measures designed for the protection of the Reich. We shall not, however, welcome measures which equate us with the communists and brand us as extremists. There is only one form of extremism and that is communism. If one fights communism, one is not an extremist but merely doing one's national duty. If any government should decide on such measures, then of course we should welcome them. We shall undoubtedly have a transitional government which, under the pretext of suppression of extremism, will try to strike at us. That we shall regard as provocation. On the other hand we are prepared to support a transitional government against the communist menace. We shall have such a government – before we ourselves seize complete power.[15] I have faith in our people, in the proletariat, in the intelligentsia and in the vast majority of officers. When Krupp, Schröder and the other captains of industry realise that we stand for order, they will be happy to be accepted into the Party. They are supporting our Movement financially but they have not the courage to allow the German

State a national government and a national leader. I have no alternative but to bring them to that decision by pressure from the people.'

B R E I T I N G : 'Would you be prepared, on the parliamentary level, to work with a national coalition government? I mean a government, of which you were speaking just now, including the bourgeoisie and the wholesome forces among the population.'

H I T L E R : 'We have founded a great party and its object is not to keep a few professional politicians in their tottering ministerial chairs. After chasing out the incompetent nobility, the French people formed their own political and State authority. If you have read *Mein Kampf*, then you will know that we have not committed ourselves on this point. We are not fighting to save the dying bourgeoisie but to guarantee the German people a new and a better life for the coming centuries – I repeat centuries. The majority of the bourgeoisie are opportunists; they are still waiting; but they will have to decide whether to march with us or go under one day along with the professional politicians. They will be forced to it by the increasing strength of our organisations. We do not doubt for a moment that, in this political struggle, there may well be another November crime.[16] Though we may not have a majority in the Reichstag, we are the spearhead of political life. At the next elections we shall win 15 million votes. Then Hindenburg, Schleicher, Hugenberg, von Papen and the financial captains of the Ruhr will realise that order cannot be established in Germany without our collaboration. Our emissaries are already in contact with their people and things are moving our way. But the situation is not yet ripe. In the political battle it always takes a long time before the will and the feelings of the people bring about a landslide. This spiritual landslide will be brought about by us and by us alone.[17] That will be the final battle and a just reward for the November betrayal. But to produce such a situation we require neither a *putsch* nor a civil war. The decision will come through our convictions and from the battle of minds. I tell you, on the day when one million SA and SS stand ready to put an end once and for all to the traitorous policy of the Social Democrats and the Centre, then the communists would loose their fighting formations upon us. We should mangle each other. But, I tell you, this will not happen. It will merely be grist to our mill, for at this juncture the Reich President, industry, finance, the officers and the ordinary citizens will realise that the day of decision is not far off. They will have no difficulty in choosing and your presence in this room shows me that the process is already under way. Let us be honest, Herr Breiting; the party politicians of the present system have no other choice. One cannot govern for ever by emergency legislation nor will it overcome the crisis. The present parties, in fact, have no programme; their leaders merely want to assure themselves a good position. How long can they go on with this policy? I tell you, the whole business is going bankrupt. If, at the next election, your Peoples Party captures one third of the 1·6 million votes it had last year, you will have done very well – I know, of course, that your politicians have been in touch with the German Nationals and my own Party. No one likes to be a failure as a politician. The clever ones are already looking for jobs in the civil service. But at the right moment we shall sweep away all these political officials. A politically-minded official, after all, can only keep his job if the government party is behind him. Look at the results achieved by the German Nationals and the Peoples Party. In 1924 the German Nationals had three times as many votes as my Party and the Peoples Party nearly twice as many. Last year (1930) the German Nationals were only half as strong as my Party and the Peoples Party only a quarter. The election figures show clearly where the future lies. Dr. Hugo may be a good salesman and have a flourishing import-export business, but he will never be able to revive Stresemann's policy. The time for that is past. A new German world policy is on the horizon. Yet now, when we need National unity, the politicians foster the separatist tendencies of the *Länder*. External political successes and national unity always go hand in hand. These successes we shall have. Look round Europe. How many countries have already lost patience with parliamentary democracy? The Kings in Europe too are no supporters of Marx. Before the Franco-Prussian War Bismarck wrote to Freiherr von Werthern (Werthern was his diplomatic representative in Bavaria – sixty years ago the German *Länder* maintained mutual diplomatic relations) that it would take five or ten years to achieve unity and even then it would be a gift of God; he added: "We may put our watches forward but that does not make the time go quicker." Suddenly the astute old Bismarck observed that, in favourable international situations, one can put the clock forward. In his day it was only necessary to abbreviate a telegram in order to be able to dictate peace in Versailles. And German unity was then an accomplished fact. We have much to be thankful to Bismarck for and much to learn from him. Yet even he committed the error of trying to rule merely with Princes and Parties. But he could do nothing else; the time was not yet ripe. Bismarck wanted a Reichstag and had the Wallot Palace built. That was his disaster. The Hohenzollerns rendered great services to Germany but that did not prevent them eventually carrying Germany to its doom. They wanted maritime supremacy and colonies on a parity with England. In fact, however, it was merely the Jews wanting to get into business; think of Bernhard Dernburg who set himself up as adviser and pretended to be related to the Hohenzollerns – not at all impossible, in fact very probable. Ilse, his wife, wrote novels in which only Jews were capable of being successful business leaders. They can put any down-at-heels business on its feet again. The brother of this Ilse Dernburg was called Max Seliger and was commissioned by the Kaiser to do the frescoes in the Gedächtniskirche and the Reichstag. Now the Social Democrat Party sits underneath

27

his work of art. This Seliger was Director of the Royal Artistic Academy in your home town and at his reserved table – in the Auerbach Keller, I think – he was always telling stories to show that only Jews were capable of being gifted artists, businessmen or politicians. Russia has already fallen into the hands of these people. Now the Jews, in league with Roosevelt, are trying to exploit the economic crisis and bring about the same result in America by socialist demagogy.[18] If, one day, they succeed in pulling the wool over the eyes of the Americans and if Germany does not contrive to regain her position, then we are all lost and Europe with us. We must hurry, in case the international situation should change. My friends and I often mull over this problem. We have five, or at the most eight, years in which to achieve our due position of political power on this continent. But the German bourgeoisie is oblivious to all this. We are therefore compelled to issue warnings. And if our warnings fall on deaf ears, the situation will become critical in Germany too. We shall then put our clocks forward also and in this internal struggle we alone are capable of victory. If in fact it comes to a crisis, the blame will lie, not at our door, but at that of the system's politicians.'

BREITING: 'Would it not be best now, before the crisis comes, to work towards co-operation between informed sections of society and the National-Socialist movement?'

HITLER: 'That would of course be the best, and if the nationalist votes and those of the Peoples Party were not being uselessly squandered, it would be easier to bring about an early national awakening. But this must first mature. We must have one or two more elections before the German Nationals realise that the Stresemann days are gone and that they have no other alternative but to form a coalition government with us.[19] And this merely leads us back to the Reichstag – the Reichstag which was guilty of shameful betrayal of its own country in 1918.[20] But this is the road we must take, first because we wish to save people the

28

bloodshed of a civil war, secondly because, in the present international situation, we cannot control Germany's future by illegal methods. We will enter the Reichstag, not from any love for this Jewish institution, but because we are realistic politicians. Once we have laid hands on power by legal means, however, we shall take care to keep it. The Reichstag can then shut its doors. We shall rule, not through the parties but through the people. The Reichstag can become a museum for future generations where we shall exhibit the machinations of world Jewry, Freemasonry, the Marxist Party and the Vatican. We will erect a memorial to the national awakening. The people's representatives will assemble for great rallies in Nuremberg and there take their decisions.[21]

'Because the nation is split the present government clings to the Reichstag, that instrument of mass deception. But we shall dispense with this system and retain our power by the will of the people. We have more than adequate intellectual equipment to create a better system.[22] To this end, however, the wreckers of the people must be rendered innocuous. We shall enter the Reichstag, not in order to govern on the English model, but because it is the legal road to power. Despite sabotage and boycott we intend to prove how competent we are. We intend to snatch the business of government out of the hands of these traders and carry through the renewal of the State. Naturally we shall welcome anyone who wishes to accompany us on this path. A great newspaper like yours can give to many other decent folk the signal to free themselves from this pack of Jews and Jewish customers. Personally I think it will be easy, but the press minds too much about its bread and butter. Nevertheless as an editor I tell you that today propaganda via the grapevine is as effective as the press. Our marches form our headlines. Our success rests solely on our electoral speeches, our propaganda and our organisations. If the press reports these objectively, it will already have done something towards the revival. Unfortunately the Jewish and communist gang frequently stand in the way. We will introduce new press legislation.[23] We shall require any journalist, diplomat or officer to prove that Aryan blood has flowed in his veins for the last six generations. The same rules will apply for North, South, East and West Germany. The Germans will have no alternative but to submit themselves unresistingly to the totality of my ideology.'

BREITING: 'From the national point of view, all right. Every German is proud to see his country united in the national sense. But, Herr Hitler, there are economic and social problems. After all, we all know that the North, which is more socialistically inclined, prefers a very different interpretation of National-Socialist principles to that of the South. I am convinced that the socialist interpretation of your programme stems from the strong tendency to agitation on the part of your propaganda chief, Herr Goebbels. If, however, the majority of your supporters are socialistically minded, the possibility remains that they will one day desert you, if promises are not kept.'

HITLER (with a scornful laugh): 'I know this gambit already. You think that I should be incapable of solving the social problems without the agreement of the bourgeoisie. You mean that my social programme is no more than demagogy thought up by my Head of Propaganda, Dr. Goebbels. As far as Dr. Goebbels is concerned, I would point out that his propaganda is not only socialist but nationalist as well. The one goes hand in hand with the other. Do not think that Dr. Goebbels' remarks are mere empty words. My Head of Propaganda is a great commander in intellectual warfare.[24] My social programme is not the expression of some personal urge for agitation on the part of someone on my staff. Once we have achieved our national, governmental and political unity, the social questions will solve themselves automatically. You must distinguish clearly between emotion and reason as far as we are concerned. In the propaganda campaign we naturally place the emotional aspect first. The economic and social problems we shall deal with completely realistically and sensibly. An army without morale will be beaten, however well equipped it may be. An army without weapons is condemned to a hero's death unless re-supply is assured. A propaganda offensive can save an army, a people, a continent. This campaign has now started and we are giving it priority. The economic and social problems only come later. I shall not do my enemies the favour of allowing the proletariat to desert me. Once we have captured the masses, things will be quite different; then nationally-minded industry and finance and the university professors will march with us in the ranks of the NSDAP. That is what the Jews and marxists are frightened of. In my Reich Propaganda Chief they see a genius of a speaker and publicist, who is not venal. It would be far easier for them without Goebbels; that I am quite prepared to believe.

'People criticise me, saying that, on aesthetic grounds, I should have chosen someone other than Goebbels as Head of Propaganda. No, gentlemen; in my view propaganda has nothing to do with how a man dresses or looks. Propaganda is a matter of the emotions, German emotions, and of unshakable faith in a future for Germany. When we have seized power I shall have a mighty official propaganda headquarters built. It will be organised as a Ministry and occupy as important a place as the Foreign Ministry or the General Staff.'[25]

BREITING: 'For this propaganda campaign which you plan, you require some economic basis and a social programme.'

HITLER: 'I will now explain my social programme to you too. In the field of economic and social policy you have something against Gregor Strasser, just as Goebbels is criticised for his propaganda. To put it quite clearly: we have an economic programme. Point No. 13 in that programme demands the nationalisation of all public companies, in other words socialisation or what is known here as socialism.

It is a bad word. It does not mean that all these concerns must necessarily be socialised, merely that they can be socialised if they transgress against the interests of the nation. So long as they do not do that, it would, of course, be criminal to upset the economy.'[26]

BREITING: 'What is your position with regard to private property? I attended the last legal conference in Leipzig and could get no satisfactory answer on this subject from your Party colleague, Feder. In bourgeois circles there is much discussion on this question of private property and I do not believe that you will register many gains in these circles unless you clarify this question. The general impression is that your speakers are deliberately vague on this point and that certain fantastic notions about universal profit-sharing show that your Party's position is a jumble of communistic and socialistic ideas. Everybody today hopes that the Third Reich's economy will provide him with that which suits his own interests. The worker, for instance, looks for profit-sharing, higher wages, state-assisted old age pensions etc. In my view your Party leaders are not doing much to clarify this matter.'

HITLER (somewhat indignantly): 'I have 8,000-10,000 speakers around the country. I cannot be held responsible for the terms in which my people put across my ideas. But it does not really matter whether my ideas are put across correctly or not; nor does it matter what the National-Socialist press or your press say on the subject. The only thing that matters is that the basic principle of my Party's economic programme should be made perfectly clear and that is the principle of authority. I want authority; I want individuality; I want everyone to keep what he has earned subject to the principle that the good of the community takes priority over that of the individual. But the State should retain control; every owner should feel himself to be an agent of the State; it is his duty not to misuse his possessions to the detriment of the State or the interests of his fellow-countrymen. That is the overriding point. The Third Reich will always retain the right to control property owners. If you say that the bourgeoisie is tearing its hair over the question of private property, that does not affect me in the least. Does the bourgeoisie expect some consideration from me? I do not take the smallest account of the bourgeoisie and its suscepti- bilities. Today's bourgeoisie is rotten to the core; it has no ideals any more; all it wants to do is earn money and so it does me what damage it can. The bourgeois press does me damage too and would like to consign me and my movement to the devil. You are, after all, a representative of the bour- geoisie. Ask your friends why they don't give me ten million marks to endow SA schools and speakers' colleges. If the bourgeoisie would make ten million marks available to me, then I would ensure that my ideas were correctly put across out in the country.[27] But your press thinks that it must con- tinuously distort my ideas.'

(Hitler becomes increasingly irate, bangs his fist on the table and screams:)

'Don't think that I care what the bourgeois press writes about me and my movement. I am no believer in the omni- potence of the press. We have become a great party without the press. I put my trust simply and solely in the spoken word.'

BREITING: 'I am sorry that you should tar the entire bourgeois press with the same brush. If you are so violently opposed to bourgeois journalists, I wonder whether discussion with you serves any purpose, Herr Hitler.'

HITLER: 'I have nothing against you personally; if I had, you would not be sitting here. I only receive journalists with whom I think a discussion would be useful. But (with a gesture of contempt) what does the entire bourgeois press mean to me and my movement? The bourgeois press throws mud at us and slanders us; it supported the ban on my speak- ing; it is opposed to my naturalisation.'[28]

BREITING: 'You should know, Herr Hitler, that the

Leipziger Neueste Nachrichten was opposed to the ban on your speaking and has demanded your naturalisation on at least a dozen occasions. I must protest against this view. I repeat, you should not tar the *Leipziger Neueste Nachrichten* with the same brush as the rest. Herr Hess has shown us your remarkably organised records. Get Herr Hess to show you the articles in our newspaper demanding your naturalisation and opposing the ban on your speaking.'[29]

HITLER: 'Good, I take note of that. But how can you then advocate a coalition with the marxists, with our deadly enemies, the Social Democrats?

BREITING: 'I am sorry, but I must correct you on this point also. The *Leipziger Neueste Nachrichten* has been a supporter of the right-wing trend in Saxony.'

HITLER (reluctantly and somewhat embarrassed): 'Well then, the *Leipziger Neueste Nachrichten* is better than it is said to be. I must read it more carefully. Hess, take care of that.'

BREITING: 'While on the subject of the press, I should like to say that the coarse intemperate tone which your own press adopts towards the bourgeois press in general and the *Leipziger Neueste Nachrichten* in particular, produces a reaction of repugnance. You wish to arouse sympathy for your national movement. You will not do so if nationally-minded journalists and politicians are insulted and have mud thrown at them by your press. I must revert to your own words here. When, for instance, I am vilified by the *Freiheitskampf*, the newspaper of your Party Gau in Dresden, do you think that that increases affection for your movement in nationalist bourgeois circles? Your NSDAP agitators are certainly no greater patriots than the *Leipziger Neueste Nachrichten*, Herr Hitler.'

HITLER: 'What some madman of an editor writes in my own press is of no interest to me. With a movement like mine, which goes the whole hog, the righteous must suffer with the wicked. We are at present the only non-marxist party determined to assert ourselves by force. We can achieve something only by fanaticism. If this fanaticism horrifies the bourgeoisie, so much the better. Solely by this fanaticism, which refuses any compromise, do we gain our contact with the masses. The German Nationalists are also anti-semitic and also have "völkisch" ideas. As far as conservatism is concerned, it was the French and British version, not the German, which showed sufficient knowledge of man-management to lead their people to victory in the war. In Germany conservatism missed its destiny and so committed a crime for which it will have to answer before history. German conservatism had completely forgotten that anything worthy of preservation must be fought for daily. It passed from the offensive to the defensive, and not merely to the defensive – it eventually allowed itself to be beaten by the Left. That is what divides us from the German Nationals today. I have a lot of time for Herr Hugenberg; I respect him highly as a patriot; but I keep saying to him: The only conservative tactics, the only correct psychological move from the national point of view, would have been to win over to the nation and the concept of the nation the alienated sections of our people. As long as we do not succeed in committing the German proletariat to the aims of the national State, the State will have no justification for existence. If you use a plane, there will be shavings. Do you think that, when we are in power, there will be no cases of hardship or injustice? No. Both in the economic and social fields there will be great hardships. We do not intend to nail every rich Jew to the telegraph poles on the Munich-Berlin road. That is nonsense. But in our "völkisch" state, which will be based on the best "völkisch" forces, the Jewish-marxist spirit has no further place.'[30]

BREITING: 'I can say nothing against this line of argument. Assuming you came to power, however, where would you find the brains to run the government administrative machine on your lines?'

HITLER (looking at me intently and speaking with

emphasis): 'I am the master mind and my secret General Staff will produce the brains we need. In any case do you not believe that, in the event of a successful revolution along my Party's lines, the brains would not come over to us in droves? Do you believe that the German bourgeoisie (scornfully), the flower of the intelligentsia, would refuse to follow us and place their brains at our disposal? The German bourgeoisie would, as usual, accept the *fait accompli*; we will do what we like with the bourgeoisie.'

(Hitler's temper suddenly rose and he became red in the face)

'We give the orders; they do what they are told. Any resistance will be broken ruthlessly. I will tolerate no opposition. We recognise only subordination – authority downwards and responsibility upwards. You just tell the German bourgeoisie that I shall be finished with them far quicker than I shall with marxism. It is the bourgeoisie's fault that the marxist disease has taken so deep-rooted a hold on our people. Marxism will be exterminated root and branch. Do you think that I shall compromise with marxism when revolution comes? I make no compromises – none whasoever. If I compromise, then marxism will revive in thirty years' time. Marxism must be killed. It is the forerunner of bolshevism. Your leading articles which try to give me advice – I laugh at them. I must steer a straight course; I must tread my chosen path unswervingly, looking neither to right nor left. Did Frederick the Great, whose picture you see here, or did Mussolini do any different? Anyway do you not believe that your bourgeoisie would prefer a national people's state to the present national system – this system which is a mere wasps' nest and which is ruining our state by its parliamentary squabbles. When once the conservative forces in Germany realise that only I and my party can win the German proletariat over to the State and that no parliamentary games can be played with the marxist parties, then Germany will be saved for all time, then we can found a German Peoples

State. Please convince Messrs Hugenberg,[31] von Papen, Dr. Hugo[32] and above all the Reich President of this.'

BREITING: 'Our newspaper is doing its best on this point. But the best brains of the bourgeoisie are afraid that one day they will be annihilated both morally and financially.'

HITLER: 'I have no wish to annihilate anybody. We need the bourgeoisie's brains to administer the new Reich. But we need only specialists, not intellectual charlatans, and these specialists must obey orders blindly. No, Germany will not fall to pieces over the establishment of the Third Reich. The dynastic foundations of Bismarck's Reich were destroyed but his creative work will be carried over into the Third Reich. Germany will survive this upheaval and the Third Reich will appear as the inevitable solution to complete the unification of the nation on a popular basis. Bismarck was mistaken in the national conclusions which he drew from the dynastic basis on which he built. He thought that, if the dynasties collapsed, the Reich would fall to pieces. He thought that German national sentiment would not survive a collapse of the dynasties. His fears were not realised; the Reich remains and if one thing is certain in Germany today, it is that assurance and hope lie in the sense of solidarity of all Germans. This sentiment is in our bones, in our flesh and blood, and is simply not to be uprooted. In Russia it was possible because the Bolshevists slaughtered their national intelligentsia. Who will fight for Marx' kolkhoz economy or for the corrupt French parliamentarians. Parliamentarianism did no good either to the Hapsburgs or the Hohenzollerns. With the suppression of that talking shop which you call the Upper House or the Reichstag and with the reorientation of the press, a new situation will arise straight away. The bells of rebirth will ring out. And at that moment we will have a ruthless reckoning with marxism.[33] Industry will at once be harnessed to the process of reconstruction. The six million unemployed will be able to earn their daily bread. The Versailles *diktat* will be swept away. A new army and a

new General Staff will arise. Your bogey Goebbels, instead
of frightening away the proletariat with his agitation, will
ensure that, both from emotion and reason, 99 per cent of
all Germans will support our policy. Six months after seizing
power we will hold a referendum such as has never been
seen before. The rest will then come automatically.[34]

'The NSDAP will ensure that the various German nationali-
ties, the German tribes, coalesce rather than go their
separate ways. Before the war, for instance, our enemies
placed all their hopes on the particularism of Bavaria; now
the Bavarians are the people who have seized upon the idea
of national renewal with special enthusiasm. This is why I
shall not leave Munich for Berlin. I intend to clean up the
Berlin Augean Stables but it must be done from here. For us
the great question mark is simply: bolshevism or fascism.
These are the two great new concepts, the great ideologies,
on which the future must decide. To me the greatest disgrace
of all is the fact that Germans could bring themselves to
support bolshevism with their money and their intelligence.
We are doing all in our power to assist the Russian Five Year
Plan, regardless of the fact that when, through our help,
that Plan begins to work, we shall face Russian dumping
on an unparalleled scale. It is infamous and disgraceful that
Germany should assist bolshevism, should support an
ideology which is the bitterest foe of a "völkisch" Germany.
We can only fight bolshevism if we confront it with a stern
ideology founded on the best forces of German nationhood,
the best forces of Christianity, the German mode of life and
the German code of ethics or morals or whatever you like
to call it.'[35]

(Hitler becomes increasingly excited and screams:)

'If we do not succeed, we shall go to the dogs and we
have no wish to go to the dogs. Every one of my 500,000
members is ready to risk his life for this.'

(Hitler gazes at me and screams:)

'Do you think I don't know what you're thinking now?

38

You are thinking that I isolate myself, that I refuse to have advisers, that I am not receptive to new ideas, that I am unapproachable and avoid discussion. (With his voice rising) I have no wish to waste time in fruitless debates about matters from which nothing emerges. I will not be diverted from my goal. I must keep to my straight course. I am concerned with my great idea. Side issues do not interest me. The remedy can come only from Munich, from Bavaria where my Movement was born. Possibly that is wrong. But rather a wrong decision, by which I stand or fall, than a half-hearted compromise.'

(Hitler becomes more and more excited)

'Berlin is no German city today; it is an international muckheap. I owe it to the 300 martyrs of my movement to steer my straight course. Do you know that I was once blind? In November 1918, when the Reds were laying Germany waste, I was in a military hospital, blinded. That was when I began to see. I shall tread my road to the end. Tell that to your rotten bourgeoisie. I intend to have one million members and I shall have them in a year. Then I will accept no more. Either I shall do it with a million or I shall never do it at all. But no one shall ever be able to say of me that I made concessions like the present-day statesmen.'

(Hitler continues to philosophise in this vein, becoming more and more excited. With difficulty I contrive to snatch a second's pause in order to interject a question raising the reparations problem)

'Naturally an end must be put to trade union policy in its present form. The trade union policy has ruined us. Between 1925 and 1928 the budget increased by 18 milliard marks as a result of the trade union policy on wages, social security, unemployment insurance etc. The two milliard annual reparations payments are nothing compared to this. If today we had no more reparations to pay, social democracy, in other words trade union policy, would immediately demand wage increases to absorb the two milliard saved.

That is nonsense and it should not be. As you will realise, I cannot say that at a public meeting.[36] Similarly I cannot express my views on private property at a popular meeting in the same way as I have done to you. We are dealing with intelligent people here. If I am not frank with you, you could not understand me either.'

BREITING: 'That is right, but in implementing these principles you will have to beware of the "man in the street".'

HITLER: 'I am no friend of the "man in the street". I match personality against the "man in the street". History is made by men, not by the masses. The masses must be led. Great historical decisions are impracticable without stern leadership of the masses. The people must be regimented into an authoritarian order of society.'

BREITING: 'In that case your ideas lead inevitably to dictatorship.'

HITLER: 'Dictatorship? Call it what you will. I am not sure whether this word should be used to describe it, but I am no friend of the amorphous mass; I am a deadly enemy of democracy which has led us into misfortune. I am also no friend of female suffrage. I am opposed to universal, equal and secret voting rights. If, however, we must continue with this tomfoolery, then we should draw what advantage we can from democracy. Women will always vote for law and order and a uniform, you can be sure of that. What nonsense – equal voting rights for the professor and the dairy maid! The élite of a people will never tolerate the masses being continuously worked up by some cunning party trickery. This system of government must be brought to an end once and for all. Democracy has killed itself with its own policy. And if the Jews persist in it, they will find themselves facing fresh pogroms which will hit them harder than those described in their biblical past. It is bad that the so-called nationally-minded bourgeoisie has not yet grasped this. According to a Norwegian friend of mine recently, Knut Hamsun has said that a memorial will be erected to those who have the courage to burn down the Storting.[37] Ask Sven Hedin what he thinks of the Russian menace. With their democracy Finland and Sweden will sooner or later be overrun by Russia. Hedin visited Hindenburg's headquarters during the war and he knows better than anybody what harm parliamentary government has done to us. The Scandinavians will opt for a real man like Hamsun rather than a financial magnate like Wallenberg or the chatter of the Swedish Social Democrats criticising our Movement. Sooner or later the "representatives of the people" will have disappeared from the French, British and German scene. At this point the masses are still dazzled and politically immature. Many honest people hope and believe that, by adhering either to the right or the left, they will gain some advantage. The élite, whether inside or outside our Party, senses that only a dictatorship can create order. The interests of the various social classes will be protected by a corporative institution, not by the Reichstag. One day hatred for the parliamentary system will be as great as its popularity appears today. Nowadays the Scandinavians bestow the Peace Prize on the protagonists of this decadent system, but the day will come when the Nobel Prize will be awarded to the man who topples these false ideals. Yes, Herr Breiting, the Third Reich will be ruled from commanders' headquarters, not by meetings of the Reichstag or professional parliamentarian Reichstag gnomes, by these tricksters who commit crimes but wear a tail coat.'[38]

(I failed to understand why Hitler was raging so bitterly against the Reichstag; initially, after all, he had said that the road to power led through the Reichstag. He seemed possessed by a rage for destruction; he was foaming at the mouth, no longer speaking clearly and so fast that I could not catch his words. I wanted to say that he seemed to be being carried away by emotional impulse and his own rhetoric. In an attempt to bring the conversation back to practical concrete matters I put the following question:)

BREITING: 'But, Herr Hitler, if you receive an absolute

majority from the people and if you wish to begin reconstruction through a coalition government, you must govern with the Reichstag.'

HITLER (he seemed to have calmed down, had wiped his mouth and was realistic again but unwilling to say anything concrete): 'We have our ideas on that also. As you know, parliaments are invariably dissolved when a government wishes to obtain the necessary majority. This manoeuvre is no monopoly of the bourgeois or marxist parties. There are two sides to that coin. The same applies to emergency legislation which is provided for under the Weimar constitution.'[39]

(I attempted to elicit some concrete answers about internal legislation but Hitler was evasive. I therefore tried to probe him about the attitude of foreign countries to his proposed dictatorial measures)

BREITING: 'What, in your view, will the outside world say and what will its attitude be if you sweep away all democratic principles?'

HITLER: 'What foreigners will say at the time is of no interest to me at this point. I have already told you that a policy must be developed in stages. Once we are in power our language to foreign countries will be dictated by the needs of the moment. We cannot discuss these diplomatic niceties today. What matters today are the general principles to which I adhere. What is advantageous to one is disadvantageous to another; what one regards as a crime, another looks upon as perfectly moral; what is right for one is wrong for another. The prerequisite is the establishment of a new, universally applicable, social and moral code.'

BREITING: 'You therefore intend the Third Reich to be constructed on an entirely new social basis?'

HITLER: 'Yes indeed, and if necessary by force – if we are challenged. I do not wish to harm the present healthy forces among the people. But age carries no priority. I have had quite enough of these gentlemen here in Bavaria.'[40]

BREITING: 'My last question, Herr Hitler: the deciding

factor is whether you achieve all this legally or illegally.'

HITLER (relaxed): 'I am quite convinced that my movement will win through legally. If my speakers out in the country talk of revolution, violence and upheaval, I cannot stop them. Eleven years ago I was still speaking to audiences of 20 National-Socialists; today there are 500,000 men united under National-Socialism in spite of emergency legislation and deception, in spite of pastoral letters and official bans. This army must be doubled; then I can win and do so legally. Make that quite clear to your friends and your readers.'

(Hitler shook hands, accompanied us to the door and said:)

'I am glad to have had this frank discussion with you. I hope that I have made a real friend.'

BREITING: 'It has all been most extraordinarily interesting to me.'

HITLER: 'If you come to Munich again and I have time, I would gladly be at your disposal once more.'

BREITING: 'This will undoubtedly be necessary for the foreign policy side of our newspaper; we would not wish our articles to leave out of account the thinking of so important a Party.'

HITLER: 'In fact we have a whole range of ideas on foreign policy. Come again so that we can talk about that.... As far as your disagreements with our Party newspaper *Der Freiheitskampf* are concerned, settle these matters with my Party comrade, Rudolf Hess. He will pass the problem on to Hans Frank, our legal adviser. If the *Leipziger Neueste Nachrichten* can find a *modus vivendi* with our Party headquarters in Leipzig, all will be set to stop the attacks.'

*   *   *

The interview had lasted nearly three hours; Hess was looking at his watch and seemed anxious to break off. He insisted that the conversation remain strictly confidential. We were a little time with Hess and I was able to see how very full Hitler's day was. All the time telephone messages were arriving from Berlin, Dortmund, Cologne, Oldenburg; couriers were coming; visitors being announced; a sleeper ticket to Oldenburg being ordered for Hitler – in short a real beehive of activity. A telephone call left Hess harassed and angry; Hitler summoned him to his study. When Hess returned, still vexed, I seized the opportunity to revert once more to the attacks in the *Freiheitskampf*, in the hope of achieving something concrete. Hess agreed with me in his estimate of these attacks and I agreed with him that I would send him the relevant pages of the *Freiheitskampf* sidelined in blue; he would then put them on Hitler's desk. It was agreed that Dr. Detig should first get in touch with Hans Frank.

*   *   *

The National-Socialist Party programme is undoubtedly vague, ambiguous and in fact adaptable to any situation. Hitler's intellect, however, is unquestionably of a far higher order than is generally assumed. His comments on the basic problems, moreover, cannot simply be written off. All the questions broached should be looked at and studied again. Straight away, however, I can say that his attitude to private property is completely unacceptable and that his comments seem to be at variance with those of other National-Socialists. Many of the economic points in the National-Socialist programme, the abolition of the 'yoke of the usurer' for instance, sound plain childish. But behind this programme and the whole imposing movement which is mapping out a completely new ideology, stands Hitler as a personality. The man is like a volcano; his flow of speech submerges his audience like a torrent; one has to watch for the moment to get a word in edgeways.

On the other hand a highly intelligent man like Hess hangs on the words of the leader he idolises with childlike faith in his eyes; there is no doubt that Hitler exerts over his staff a semi-hypnotic influence of almost inconceivable proportions. Unlike Spengler, therefore, one must be careful not to underestimate him. The man has personality of a really high order. One must not forget the milieu from which he comes – casual labourer, painter's mate, small-time artist. Nevertheless Hitler does not give the impression of behaving like an upstart, as some people try to say of him. He is, of course, vastly temperamental and his outbursts are feared – I was told that sometimes he rages round the Brown House like a madman. When he feels let down (by Otto Strasser for instance), he is said to burst into tears.[41] Hysteria perhaps. The significant point is that people fear him and no one dares to make fun of him in any way. For those who do not know him he undoubtedly has a tendency to megalomania; he is already playing the future dictator and is undoubtedly both desirous and determined to be the German Mussolini. On the other hand he is, to a certain extent, both happy-go-lucky and impulsive; both these traits were in evidence during our conversation and they came as a pleasant surprise. His incalculability is initially irritating, but fascinating at the same time; this makes him sometimes prone, I believe, to violent fluctuations which embarrass his associates and cause his enemies to say that he is of no great calibre and incapable of taking the right decisions at the right moment. His egotism is undoubtedly enormous and exaggerated – that is clear from his talk with its continual 'I intend, I intend, I intend'. The effect is as though his entire energy was concentrated into one single iron determination. He is undoubtedly a neurasthenic, highly excitable, and an excessively temperamental speaker. On the other hand he looks like a man of determination who could be brutal; if, as people say, he was once a weak man with a touch of the artist in him, all I can say is that he certainly does not give that impression now.

His features, his large shining black eyes[42] and the small dark moustache like a centrepiece beneath his nose give an impression of determination; his strong chin shows very great energy. As he speaks he frequently grimaces as if he would like to crush his opponent with his teeth. This continuous effort of willpower plays on his nerves and so he is today undoubtedly a highly over-excitable and highly strung man. Nevertheless, of all the politicians whom I have met personally in recent years (Stresemann included) Hitler is the man who makes the strongest impression as a personality.

* * *

In discussion with Herr Herfurth it was decided that Dr. Detig should carry on the discussions with Dr. Frank to settle our quarrel with the *Freiheitskampf*. We would disregard the insulting remark that we were Jewish lackeys and would not file any judicial complaint. It was further decided that I should have another interview with Hitler, in the strictest secrecy and without the knowledge of any member of the editorial staff. At this interview I should seek to convince him of the goodwill he was forfeiting among the bourgeoisie by failing to stop his attacks. Said Herfurth: 'We must try everything somehow to make this man a parliamentarian.'

Second Interview with Hitler, June 1931

At the second meeting early in June 1931 there were present:
Rudolf Hess, Hans Frank (only for the first part of the discussion), Adolf Hitler and Richard Breiting. The shorthand
text gives no date for the meeting. It is possible that a typewritten transcript was prepared at the time but this can no
longer be found. A remark by Hitler – 'as I told you a month
ago' – shows that it must have taken place early in June.
There is also nothing to show where the meeting was held,
but it may be assumed that, like the first interview, the venue
was the Munich headquarters. The first page of the shorthand may also have been lost, since the text begins as
follows:

HITLER: 'The press must be harnessed into the service
of the community and should no longer serve private interests.
We want a respectable press as I told you a month ago. Dr.
Frank here has told me that directives have already been
issued to the *Freiheitskampf* to settle this dispute.'

FRANK: 'This does not depend solely on the solution we
propose but also on the attitude of the *Leipziger Neueste
Nachrichten*.'

BREITING: 'I trust you will excuse me, Herr Hitler, but
I feel I must say to you that your ideas and your statements
will impress primarily the discontented. We all know, however, that once the crisis has been overcome, these people
can be diverted in other directions. Your unshakeable faith
seems to be founded upon a forecast of the future which
assumes that chance and good fortune will be on your side;
you underestimate the capabilities of your enemies. Would
it not be better to adopt a policy benefiting both the bour-

geoisie and your party at the same time? The German people needs a period of political peace.'

HITLER (indignantly): 'A battle of the mind cannot be fought with faith alone; reason must play its part. In addressing the masses we must appeal to their emotions, their faith; in our councils, however, hopeful speculation founded on faith has no place. Everything is weighed up realistically. We do not underestimate our enemy; we know what the system's politicians are capable of. Nevertheless their machine is worn out and cannot now be overhauled. We proceed by mathematically accurate planning and with Prussian precision. We look at our successes and failures quite realistically and draw the lessons from them. We do not allow ourselves to be deluded by exaggerated optimism. The fact that we can look forward to the future with confidence is due to our experience and the corrective produced by our failures. We work in stages and we reject any method which has once proved itself wrong.

'The right weapons must be brought into action at the right moment. Anyone familiar with the thinking of Clausewitz and Schlieffen knows that military strategy can also be used in the political battle. The first step is to find out about one's enemy, the second is preparation and the third the assault. You may be sure that we shall make no further mistakes.

'We cannot dabble in every parliamentary manoeuvre. We are counting only on the German Nationals. But they are not yet ready to form a coalition government with us. You need have no fear; we shall not proceed chaotically or without a plan. We have available a taut, hierarchically organised Party machine. I am giving away no secret when I tell you that our State will be similarly organised. We have been able to create iron leadership, a Party and a Movement; we shall also be able methodically to seize power, equally methodically to construct a State and methodically to destroy the Versailles *diktat*. We are no revolutionaries relying on the support of the proletarian riff-raff. My Party comrade Goebbels once put it very well; he said that only the chaotic Russian spirit could have given birth to a Bakunin. Murder as a method was used against us before we used it ourselves; there are already 300 names on our list of martyrs. The anarchist groups are paid to commit acts of terrorism against me and my closest associates. As intermediaries the financiers use intellectuals, individuals with no roots in the community. We are watching all this rabble closely and at the right moment we shall strike against them ruthlessly. When the day of reckoning comes, we shall claim our due reward. There will be no St. Bartholomew's Night; everyone will have to answer for his actions according to German law.[1] But this method – decision and use of the law – will not be approved by our own people alone; other peoples will also defend themselves against the bolshevist and Jewish chaos, for we must make our determination plain to the world. We have already gained friends abroad because we have made clear our position against bolshevism and world Jewry. We will tolerate no lackeys of the Jews in our midst – whether in the press, the economy or the diplomatic service.

'As early as 1914, after volunteering for service, I read in Philipp Stauff's book of the brazen incitements published in the German press at the behest of Jewish tyranny.[2] The Jews could deploy because the State placed no obstacles in their way. Their activities were not confined to Germany but extended over all countries. A hundred years ago Heine went to France to mobilise people there against the German "Thunder". When we come to power we shall see many Heines abroad labelling us as the Four Horsemen of the Apocalypse. That Jewish poet was right in one thing, however – that in our case action follows thought as quickly as thunder follows lightning.[3] Even now we must think how we can protect the French and British peoples against such manoeuvres. Our Foreign Section has taken major precautionary measures and we have no intention of aping the

Kaiser's colonial policy. Herr Dernburg's policy is long since dead. On the contrary we shall propose to the British that we protect their Empire with our soldiers. The worst defeat of all would be the loss by the Whites, the British and Dutch, of their key positions on the various continents.

'My closest adviser, with us here now, can assure you how firmly we believe that we must be long-term allies of England. That is the essential guarantee of peace in Europe and the world.'

HESS (emphatically): 'Our Führer has always insisted that our most natural friend and ally is England. Think of England's world geographic situation and Germany's central position in Europe.'[4]

HITLER: 'Before we deal with these foreign policy questions, I would like to say something more on the press. We should be happy if we had settled our quarrel with all newspapers. I would like to stress once more that, as we stand at present, we have no wish to subject the press to control. We have neither the resources nor the authority. When the time comes our organisation will take care of information policy and the press. Havas, Reuter, Associated Press and such like will not be able to put spokes in the wheel of our struggle for the spirit of the people. The so-called great reporting press in New York, London, Amsterdam, Paris, Brussels, Copenhagen and Stockholm will be compelled to report on us in the way that suits us. They will dance to our tune since their sensation-mongering public demands news. And we will give them news in any quantity they like. The publishers' ring will lose its head. At present some secret orchestrator is located somewhere in New York, London or Paris. Our news will shut him up. You are a journalist and you understand what I mean. Atrocity propaganda was able to soften up the Kaiser. I shall mobilise the entire country against the atrocity-mongers. The Jews will be the losers, not me.'

BRIETING: 'Herr Hitler, what you are saying in effect

is it not, is that the international press has clubbed together to boycott your organisation and that this counter-organisation is run by Jews?'

HITLER: 'Precisely. What is more, this club includes the German press and radio, since we are not yet masters of the State. We cannot deal with this situation since we are living today under a police and administrative system which is controlled by the great monopolies and largely related to Jews. This is where the headlines are written; this is where you find the supreme arbiters of art and the economy. Lies are printed and people believe them. It is very difficult to get the truth through to the masses. Our fighting paper, the *Völkischer Beobachter*, has only made slow progress. In 1920 we had a circulation of 6,000, in 1922 18,000 and now it is about 140,000. On the day when we seize power our newspaper will undoubtedly be able to print a million copies. There will be no need then for us to act the new broom; the "völkisch" policy will automatically impose itself on the press. The all-party coalition directed by the marxist, Jewish and Jesuit cesspit, which now makes poisonous attacks on us in every newspaper, will burst like a soap-bubble – and not because the people's thoughts and actions are opportunist but because their eyes will have been opened. Ten years ago Dietrich Eckart maintained that it was not the people who were opportunist but the bourgeoisie and their politicians.[5] Nothing has occurred meanwhile to change this. They merely bicker about ministerial seats and salaries. We will give them both, even if I have to give up my pay as a Cabinet member.[6] Eckart was an outstanding writer and thinker. My friends thought him eccentric but I was convinced that in the future we needed legions of men like Eckart. History is invariably made by individuals, by geniuses. But however great the leader's genius, he must have his work publicised. A people can be brought to realise its historic mission only by a small group of determined men. For this purpose clean, harmonious, unified leadership is far more effective than a squalid coalition of various parties drawing its support from the press cesspit. Enemy intelligence will find no possibilities of worming its way into our ranks. Cosmopolitan parasites live off the opportunism of the bourgeoisie. The only danger confronting us is that of communism since it is the only one of our opponents to possess an ideology. It is also the only one which can face us with a mass fighting organisation. Communism is the Enemy Number One of our organisation and of the bourgeoisie.

'We alone can save the disintegrating bourgeoisie from this foe. The Jews may utilise this fighting organisation against us. They will certainly try. Our national bourgeoisie is as opportunistically minded as its Jewish allies. We wish to say quite frankly that if, in this struggle for the German people's existence, the Jews ally themselves with the communists, they will be attacked. They sense this and so they are indirectly filling our Party coffers. Social democracy is not a class-conscious organisation. Should they form a coalition with the communists against us, they too will be mortally wounded. We work with mathematical precision. We may refer to your jumble as a system but what we mean thereby is simply your anarchy. You are in no position to construct a system; your system is merely permanent disintegration.'

BREITING: 'But, Herr Hitler, you cannot blame me for the present government's policy. Though he is a member of our party, I am no more responsible for Curtius and his foreign policy than I am for Joseph Wirth's internal political measures. I have always advocated a right-wing policy in Saxony. I sent Herr Hess a cutting from the communist *Volkszeitung* attacking me and calling me the "real dictator" of Saxony. It is due to me that the marxists are not in control in Saxony and that an unimpeded right-wing policy is being pursued.'

HITLER: 'But this has not prevented your party friends

in Thuringia from attacking Frick and my friends. You must persuade your party to withdraw its support in future from this government of national debilitation. Brüning considers the 6½ million National-Socialists to be insignificant. If so many patriotically minded men can be disregarded and government carried on by emergency legislation, one might as well dissolve parliament and draw up a new constitution. This government has already been at it for fourteen months. And what is the result? Both internally and externally we face the greatest dangers today. A system of terror is in control; there is no character – to say nothing of the will to lead. Brüning has set himself the object of dividing the nationalist forces. Look at Schiele and his people who have deserted Hugenberg and call themselves Popular Conservatives.[7] They want to rule with marxist support. The Finance Minister talks about savings. But this saving will lead to catastrophe. And Schiele's agricultural policy will lead to the breakdown of agriculture. Curtius calls himself a European but wants to conduct a continental policy through the League of Nations. Until we have formed a Peoples State and put our internal policy in order, Germany will have no success with the League. The battle will be fought at home, not in the League of Nations. All these gentlemen want to do is to divide, divide and divide again. We cannot overcome our internal political difficulties with Groener or Wirth, with Dietrich or Schiele. On the contrary. Let's just look at the figures.'

(Hitler takes up a typewritten sheet of paper of which I take a copy later)

'In January 1930 there were 3,217,000 unemployed. Of these 2·5 million drew national assistance. In February of this year there were 4·9 million unemployed, of whom 4·4 million drew national assistance. If we include the 300,000 or 400,000 on short time, the figure has probably risen to 5·5 or 6 million during this conversation.[8] How can this problem be solved? Certainly not by dividing people up into those entitled to unemployment insurance whose entitlement to benefits has expired and those dependent on national assistance – who get nothing at all. Of our labour force of 16 million, 6 million are now unemployed – more than a third. Of these unemployed one-fifth receive nothing at all and 4·5 million live on public money. A colossal civil service machine is required to administer these people who would like to work. We should not be surprised if, under these conditions, the marxists are making increasing progress. At the Reichstag elections of last year the communists for the first time scored more votes in Berlin than the Social Democrats – communists 739,235, Social Democrats 738,094. What sort of a capital is that with the marxists in the majority? Moreover of 2·7 million votes cast in Berlin the communists and Social Democrats combined scored 1·5 million.[9] Don't forget that in Russia 50,000 bolshevists available at the right moment were enough to seize power. The State must now go on its knees to foreign countries for a year's postponement of war debts. And what good will that do? Meanwhile the government may decide to adopt a communist policy and communists will be allowed to club us down in the streets. The government has just banned the Hitler Youth Gau Rally in the Rhineland. The Jews, of course, welcome this policy. And Dr. Goebbels, our Party comrade, is sentenced to a month's imprisonment for slandering the Jews.[10] We are now supposed to save so that we cannot be reproached for failure to pay reparations. When I think that Hindenburg, our great commander, is going along with all this, my heart sinks. Saxony in fact shows us where all this is leading; there the Landbund has come out against Schiele. We recruited 36,000 new members throughout the Reich during the month of March, and they are still coming along. At the elections in Schaumburg-Lippe we increased our share of the vote by 35 per cent. All the indications are that nothing can stop our progress. The populace must eventually realise this. If I am reproached for acting brutally, I can tell you that in politics decisions on power stand or fall, reach historic heights – or fail to do so – only if they are implemented by purely German and brutal methods. That can only be achieved by a totally German power policy.'

BREITING: 'Could we not improve the parliamentary system?'

HITLER: 'You must not harbour these illusions. For good legislation we need a good government but we do not need a smooth-running parliament. We have plenty of time to think about the form in which we will ratify legislation. As early as 1921 I wrote in the *Völkischer Beobachter* that, in order to rouse the masses, we must preach battle. Once on the move, the mass of a people does not need a parliament; it needs leadership. The day is coming ever closer when the masses must have decent government. The people will then be glad if the parliamentary cesspool is blown sky-high. We have always been sounding the trumpet for battle against the whole parliamentary rabble, against the system, and we do not intend to stop halfway. We must create an entirely new situation, so that we can reconstruct the press, the schools, the building industry and our political as well as our military might. Just as this reawakening requires a new press, so does our country require a new form of architecture.[11] We shall also ensure that schools and universities, art and music are harnessed to the service of the people.[12] German cities should have a new look, the German countryside be changed by architectonic landscaping. Once we place our manpower and our industrial potential at the service of reconstruction, miracles will occur. Monumental buildings will tower over the squalid mob. We shall not build tenement houses; the external character of a region or a city will be determined by its economic and spiritual requirements. We will bequeath mighty works to our successors. We need no Prussian Academy of Art with its propensity for crazy architecture and decadent painting.[13] Even before the war a perceptive art critic like Stauff was demanding that the decadent painters be consigned to the lunatic asylum and their paintings destroyed instead of being hung in museums. Their crazy stuff ended up in the museum because someone thought he could earn money thereby. Literature, the theatre and the cinema will be used as means of educating the people, supported by the press and the radio. In *Mein Kampf* I have already stressed the importance of art and architecture. What has the monarchy bequeathed to us? Ugly buildings like the Kaiser's palace and a host of other insignificant buildings. Or do you think the Wallot Palace beautiful?'[14]

BREITING: 'I do not find it particularly beautiful, Herr Hitler. But it is, nevertheless, one of our most interesting buildings. You yourself said that the Wallot Palace could be turned into a museum when Germany had no further need of a parliament.'

HITLER: 'I tell you frankly, Herr Breiting, good museums require new buildings and new cities. The Wallot Palace is a symbol of our decadence. It is a hotch-potch consisting of four clusters of Parthenon-like columns mixed up with a Roman basilica and a Moorish fortress – the whole thing giving the impression of a vast synagogue. I tell you, the Reichstag is an extraordinarily ugly building, a meeting house, a talking shop for the representatives of the degenerate bourgeoisie and the deluded working class. Both the building and the institution which it houses are a disgrace to the German people, and one day they must go. In my opinion the sooner this talking shop is burnt down,[15] the sooner will the German people be freed from foreign influence. I can assure you of one thing, Herr Breiting: never will I set foot in that abode of traitors.[16] If we do not succeed in creating something new, all that present-day Germany will have to bequeath to coming generations will be five or six unprepossessing skyscrapers and thousands of department stores and hotels, all intended to fill Jewish moneybags.'

BREITING: 'I understand you very well, Herr Hitler,

but you must admit that it will be difficult for people to agree when they are told that everything laboriously constructed by previous generations should now be destroyed.'

HITLER: 'Naturally this will not happen overnight. The people must be educated first. But to create something new, we must rub the slate clean. We will turn the old cities into new ones; this depends not only on the State resources which we shall make available, but also on recent traffic developments. A new Munich, Nuremberg, Berlin, Hamburg and Cologne will arise. The centuries-old cathedral town of Leipzig will become an artistic and commercial centre for the entire continent. We will have all Europe's books printed there. A mighty and entirely new road network will extend all over Germany, so that foreigners will gape.[17] We must have working men, not unemployed. You will see that our labour force will soon be too small for our plans.[18] To carry out these mighty plans, designed for eternity, we have no need of parties or their temples. We have confidence in our workers, in our intelligentsia and in our soldiers. I include soldiers because we must protect our *lebensraum*. We need arable land and foreign workers. Under the shackles of Versailles it cannot be done. We cannot go on like this. The views on Versailles circulated by the bourgeois parties have only one object: to weaken the National-Socialist Party and divorce from it the patriotically-minded intelligentsia and the officer corps. But we shall ensure that our teachers, professors, engineers, doctors and officers once more find their way into the *völkisch* movement. We have more adherents in the officer corps than Herr Schleicher dreams of. We have no wish to destroy everything; there is a sound Prussian core in the Reichswehr and it could be the seed of a mighty oaktree.'

(After these general statements on cultural and party political questions Hitler turned to the international situation and his programme for the future. Hans Frank left the meeting)

57

HITLER: 'We must look facts in the face. One day the Soviet Union will be a giant power capable of over-running Germany and Europe. We must not lose sight of this fact. I am no bitter opponent of communism simply because the concept did not stem from me; when I was a worker I busied myself with socialist or, if you like, marxist literature. It all sounds splendid but when it comes to putting it into practice, it is not the proletariat which takes the decisions; the strings are pulled by some mysterious intellectuals on behalf of high finance. The name of your present day Moses is Marx.

'This is why they tolerate the activities of the communist party. In England and France, Holland and Belgium, Germany and Austria it is the way to pervert the masses, cling to world domination and play the colonial policeman. The British Labour Party pretends to be the opposition, but with its socialistic phrases it helps the "One Hundred Families" to dominate large parts of the world. There are no communists in England because the British bourgeoisie and plutocracy do not need them. Since they exploit the labour force and the colonies, they can afford to throw the proletariat a few crumbs from their rich man's table.

'We must complete our reconstruction before the Soviet Union becomes a world power, before the three million square miles possessed by the United States turns into an arsenal for world Jewry. These two colossi are still asleep. When they wake up, that is the end of it for Germany. In the Soviet Union, of course, things did not turn out as Marx foresaw. The Jews let the build-up of socialism slip through their fingers. This is proved by the struggle between Stalin and Trotsky. This struggle is no ideological disagreement; it is a battle between the Jewish intelligentsia, which played an important part at the time of the revolution, and the other peoples of the Soviet Union. This quarrel will not be settled for a long time. With his present methods Stalin will not succeed. The West, however, which is anti-German, needs the Stalinist form of Soviet Union as a means of pressure against a reawakened Germany. Even if, in our propaganda, we equate our communists with those of the Soviet Union, they are in fact two different worlds. In the German communist party there are forces and tendencies representing their own interests and struggling for their own existence. We have no need to be frightened of intervention by the Russians for a long time to come. Between Germany and Russia there is still a chauvinist Poland. We have no need to fear America either. Isolationist forces are strong and they have no intention of meddling in European affairs too soon. The Kellogg Pact concluded three years ago must have some significance.[19] After this the French will not be able to meddle in other states' affairs by force.

'The basic principles of our foreign policy are clear and they should cause no fear to anyone. In the first place we want to bar the road to the communists so that the tragic events of 1918 cannot be repeated. Secondly we wish to pursue a stable government policy – and that in all fields of government business. Thirdly we wish to undertake no commitments which we might not be able to fulfil. Fourthly we wish to establish a sound orderly relationship with France. On this last point I must say something to you. France should not regard the Berlin government as her tool but as an equal partner representing a great neighbouring state. There are too many influences at work in Paris thinking exclusively of reparations, whether it be Briand, Herriot or Laval. These gentlemen must understand that they will get nowhere with their occupation policy. You know that the monarchy has just fallen in Spain – and already Jews are taking governmental decisions. We can hope for nothing from these French politicians. New forces must first appear. "Action française"[20] and the ex-servicemen understand our position better. Unfortunately as a financial centre Paris too is completely dominated by Jews. The socialist party is also whipping up feeling against our movement because its leaders are Salomon Grumbach and Léon Blum.'

BREITING: 'But, Herr Hitler, one should not see Jewish conspiracies behind every tree. Everywhere there are ideological struggles and people must work out their solutions in concert. What I mean is that nothing will be achieved in Germany merely by whipping up anti-Semitism.'

HITLER (indignantly): 'What are we to fight world Jewry with, then? Tell me that. This riffraff, this rabble from the East, is ready for any crime. I am fully informed of the agitation against my movement in Paris, London, and New York. I repeat: they want to divide people, buy them and bribe them – and finally get the communists to murder us. I must be quite blunt about the impression I have of them. Why should not Rosenberg fight the Freemasons? The Lodges have become tools of the Jews. I know what Grumbach says and writes in Paris about me and my movement. *Vorwärts* is an inflammatory Jewish rag. The French Jews would like to keep Germany in the position of a vassal by means of the Centre and Socialist Parties. While we were still fighting at the front the Socialist Party was already spying for the French. Have you read the revelations of Sir Borden(!) the Canadian Prime Minister?[21] Everything that happened in Germany was transmitted to London, Paris and New York. I know this in detail. By banning the NSDAP they want to open the door to marxism. Today they capture Thuringia, tomorrow the whole of Germany. Thank God there are still people in New York and London who think differently. Grumbach wants to maintain reparations and French military superiority. Rothermere, on the other hand, would like to cancel war debts. There are decent people in America too – primarily Hoover of course.[22] But woe to us if, one day, the Jewish string-pullers set their puppets in motion. America did not sign the peace treaty of course but she has invested three or four milliard in Germany. People in the City of London are very interested in my movement's aims. Early this year Mussolini appealed to the

Americans. America can force the European powers to alter the peace treaty. Wilson carries a great responsibility. America entered the war and is responsible for the present situation. For political reasons England and Italy will be favourable to the new Germany. Alliance with Germany will solve the future of the British Commonwealth. It is therefore in America's interest that Germany should regain her honour and dignity, that she should not be hamstrung by reparations and war debts. Eighty per cent of all our obligations stem from reparations. This leads to new burdens for Germany. We are burdened with high interest rates. That leads to economic collapse. But instead of listening to the voice of reason, the word is now once more going round in America that our movement could be a danger to the world. This is the way new statesmen get to the top. I can tell you now who the next Presidential candidate will be and there is no difficulty in guessing what he thinks about Germany. We have no alternative. We must fight in the open – in the way they fight us. Should there be a party truce they must give proof of their goodwill. But their evil intentions are shown by their frenzied efforts to keep the German government in power even though the country is being devoured by the communists meanwhile. The Jews should tremble before us, not we before them. How many Jews are there here in Germany actually? And what an influence they exert! There are forces in New York supporting Roosevelt and they are becoming increasingly worried over the fate of the continent of Europe. Roosevelt and his political string-pullers will certainly give no great welcome to a reawakened Germany.[23] They reckon that, should it ever come to a showdown, the battle will be between the Germans and the Slavs. But we shall know how to protect our *lebensraum* without war. Roosevelt and his ilk will get no chance to repeat the policy of Wilson. We shall isolate Russia before she becomes a danger to us. We shall rouse the anti-communist forces in all countries. If we do not do so, one day we shall be threatened both militarily and politically by this bolshevist Russia. The political threat will be there on the very day we seize power. Even today, therefore, we are thinking of an anti-Comintern policy in all countries. Once Germany is provided with a modern army, the Soviet Union will never be a danger to her. But this Weimar Germany will be an easy prey for the bolshevists.

'For Moscow danger threatens once we become a political power in Europe. For tactical reasons, therefore, they are ready to divorce themselves from their revolution and form an alliance with the Jews and the bourgeoisie. Our World War enemies – England, France, Poland, the Little Entente – will try to come to some agreement with Russia in order to stop our revival. We are already thinking of all these complications which might and will arise.'

BREITING: 'How do you propose to avoid these complications?'

HITLER: 'Once we have become a political power, we can assume obligations. England and France must look facts in the face, for on the day when Russia becomes a great industrial country, with her reservoir of manpower and her geographical position she will become a menace not only to the Reich but to England and France as well. We must take the necessary measures to protect our people and its historic influence in the East; the Baltic States, lying between Germany and Russia, must come under our influence, not that of the Soviets. It is in the interests of Italy, England, France, Belgium, Holland and the Scandinavian countries to keep bolshevism as far from their frontiers as possible. Once this east European area, called "Inter-Europe" by certain journalists, has become a German military protectorate, the destruction of this colossus with feet of clay – should it oppose German interests – will be a mere bagatelle.'[24]

BREITING: 'Do you not think that the West would intervene against such an expansionist policy?'

HITLER: 'We do not propose to subdue these countries by war. The economic, social, ethnic and political situation in Europe will necessitate the rapid solution of urgent questions such as the relationship of Austria to Germany and Germany's relationship to Czechoslovakia and the Corridor. Once we have regained our strength and are able to defend ourselves, England and France will be only too glad to find a *modus vivendi* with us. We are no longer living in 1923 when the French and Belgians could march into the Ruhr. We will talk to them about it in the League of Nations. Sensible people realise that we cannot guarantee our security with an army of 100,000 men. We shall face them with the question whether to ally themselves with us to construct a new order or with the bolshevists to descend into anarchy and ruin. We have no intention of threatening British mastery of the seas or the French colonial empire. Certain things will automatically change in these countries because the people will learn from our example. They too will have to defend themselves against Jewish and marxist intrigues.'[25]

BREITING: 'I have no wish to interrupt you but I would merely like to observe that your struggle has already lasted twelve years and we are still a long way from seeing your aims fulfilled. I believe that this strategy, which you also set out in *Mein Kampf*, is an obstacle to your progress. The bourgeoisie views it with scepticism and is afraid of complications.'

HITLER: 'When I celebrated my 42nd birthday a few weeks ago I assured my friends that in ten years' time all Germany's internal and external political problems would have been solved. I can only repeat that to you. With our 20-million labour force and our technical heritage we only require to make a financial effort over four to five years to achieve military power; that power will draw a red pencil through Versailles and guarantee the German people in this period the space and place on the continent of Europe to which race and history entitle them.[26] The Nordic Germanic component is still there; it has by no means been lost; countries such as Holland, Flanders, Luxemburg, Switzerland, Norway, Sweden, Denmark, the Baltic Germans, the Danube basin and as far east as the Volga will awaken automatically.[27] We have no wish to pick a quarrel with Italy or present-day France over the Tyrol, Alsace or Lorraine. All that will solve itself. We have no wish to be like Austria and Italy, quarrelling with some other country over a few thousand square miles. On the day when Italy declares herself willing to protect our southern flank against England the South Tyrol question will to all intents and purposes be solved. We would rather see Italy in North Africa than France. But we shall have to pursue a realistic policy. Mussolini is inspired by the same ideals as we are. One day the old Europe must disappear. We have never accepted the 1918 betrayal – and we never shall.'

BREITING: 'With your policy might you not be labelled as a revanchist and is it not possible that the other countries might get together in an anti-German coalition?'

HITLER: 'Revanchist policy – call it what you will. But we shall not behave like a bull in a china shop. We shall proceed legally and by stages. I know that many bourgeois circles fear that I might let loose a war. You can reassure your friends; we wish to come to some agreement with the Hundred English families. We could even hold discussions with the Vatican and with Roosevelt and his crew; if necessary there could be peace with Stalin for a time.'[28]

BREITING: 'Will not people see some contradiction between what you say and what you do?'

HITLER: 'I like the frank way in which you express your opinion. At the start of our talk I stressed that I wanted frankness. Though not one of us, you are a friend; you proved it by supporting my naturalisation. Most people whom I interview are under Party discipline and are working in accordance with directives. Many of my non-Party visitors are sycophants, so that I need frank discussion. Well-founded criticism and exchanges of view are very useful. Otherwise how should we make progress? When you tell me that I am involving myself in policy contradictions, I must point out to you that this will occur even more frequently in the future. We old soldiers know that withdrawal to a better position does not mean that the battle has been lost. A political or diplomatic reconciliation may provide us with better jumping-off positions, from which we shall eventually succeed. In politics, as in strategy, the only successful commander is the one who faces his enemy with unforeseen situations. Retreat or contradiction may be part of a plan. Both internally and externally all our policy will proceed according to plan. Each operation will be carried out at the right moment. Our policy is so designed that it can be adjusted at any moment. Strategically nothing will be improvised, nothing can surprise us since we have thought of everything. We shall compel other people to face unexpected situations. We have indeed learnt much in the past. What concerns us now is that the people should have confidence in our far-sightedness and in our march to victory. We do not philosophise with every Tom, Dick and Harry about what we propose to do and what not to do. In speaking to you thus I would like to convince you once and for all that we really have thought of everything and forgotten nothing. Our movement has already acquired friends in Rumania, Bulgaria, Sweden, Norway, Holland and even in France and England. We are living in a revival period for the nationalist bourgeoisie and for the proletariat as well. I interview people here from Denmark and Holland, decent people who tell me openly of their misgivings. Look at conditions in Amsterdam and Copenhagen. These outsize urban heads on little agricultural bodies are collapsing under the weight of their own bourgeoisie. What a parasite the Dutch and Danish bourgeoisie is for their workers and farmers. As I see from an economic report, however, there are vast areas in the East

yielding far less than one would expect. The young Dutch-
men and Danes would count themselves lucky to be able
to go off to the East as colonisers along with the Germans.
Let the British and French make no mistake – Czechoslovakia is a rotten apple; the Slovaks are treated life serfs. In
1929 King Alexander set up a military dictatorship. Look
how the oppressed peoples in Jugoslavia react. In Rumania
it is no better. To say nothing of the discontent among our
Austrian brethren. A year after we have taken over power
Austria will join us of her own free will.'[29]

(Hitler falls silent and seems to be thinking. He goes on
in a calm voice. His voice has altered and is quite soft. I
admire his capacity to gear his expression to what he is
saying)

HITLER: 'I have much to thank my father for. He was
a customs official. He knew Austrians and Bavarians, Germans and Slavs, Italians and French. For him Austria was
always just a part of the great German Fatherland. Even
as a child I heard my father say that Vienna was ruled by
a clique, a mongrel crew which had collected in the capital.
Later I was able to check this for myself. This hotch-potch
of so-called liberals could not be expected to have any
leaning towards a pan-German policy. Their cultural policy
was Austrian in name only. What is good enough for Prussia
is good enough for Austria too. There can be no true racial
policy which does not safeguard our biological Aryan roots.
We intend one day to give this ideological principle the
force of law. Even today our youth is crying with good
reason: Germany awake, down with Jewry. In Vienna I
learnt to hate the Jews. Any license given the Vienna Jews
was tantamount to an increase in the number of destructive
parasites. In Munich or Berlin, Hamburg or Vienna I shall
judge the depth of people's love for their country by the
degree of hatred which they show to this rabble. It is our
job to tear up these newspaper rags which prophesy our
downfall and throw them into the dustbin; similarly it is

our duty to close and disinfect cinemas and theatres which promote the decay of our youth. Vienna has turned itself into the metropolis of decay and filth. People there sponsor books opposing the reawakening of Germany. Obviously we shall burn this rubbish and have a clean-up in Vienna as in Berlin. I would only like to say one thing to you, Herr Breiting: our people has produced great masters of speech, writing, painting and stone-masonry. The greatness of a nation, however, will be judged not by the counterfeit cultural standards of present-day civilisation but by its overall achievements, the eternal values and the eternal force which have brought forth great men.[30] I intend to throw our innate qualities into the world scales. This I regard as my mission and, in the name of these immortal virtues of our nation, I shall ensure that Austria returns home and once more becomes a happy German country. I really wanted to be an architect. The Vienna Jews knew how to stop that. They were wrong because now they have a politician on their hands. For a long time afterwards I dreamed of writing political books. But I had not the time. I wanted to write books in order to tell the people how, by their own efforts, they could make their position so impregnable that they need never fear war any more. But they shut me up in Landsberg. Now they have got a book, *Mein Kampf*, which overshadows all ordinances, bans and imprisonments. If they try to suppress my movement, they will provoke a civil war and we of the swastika flag will be the survivors, not the gentlemen from Grunewald and Wannsee. What do you think of my book, Herr Breiting?'

BREITING: 'It is undoubtedly a symbolic work. It points the way for your movement but unfortunately your opponents do not take it seriously enough. I have learnt much from your book and it is for this reason that I am paying you this second visit.'

HITLER: 'You have said that it is of significance for my movement, Herr Breiting. I say that it is of historic and decisive importance for Germany and the entire Aryan race. Beethoven, Schiller, Goethe, Treitschke, Nietzsche came and went but nothing changed. The Frenchman Gobineau and the Englishman [Houston Stewart] Chamberlain were inspired by our concept of a new order – a new order, I tell you, or if you prefer, an ideological glimpse into history in accordance with the basic principle of the blood. We do not judge merely by artistic or military standards or even by purely scientific ones. We judge by the spiritual energy which a people is capable of putting forth, which will enable it in ten years to recapture what it has lost in a thousand years of warfare. I intend to set up a thousand-year Reich and anyone who supports me in this battle is a fellow-fighter for a unique spiritual – I would almost say divine – creation. At the decisive moment the decisive factor is not the ratio of strength but the spiritual force employed. Betrayal of the nation is possible even when no crime has been committed, in other words when a historic mission has not been fulfilled. It is not the calling of every honest man to lead an empire. Our need is not the accidental appearance of some clever man or the administrative capability of some respectable lawyer, but the civic and political courage of an entire generation. The law must adapt itself to this imperative. Only a far-sighted people can act as a spur to history. The men called to lead a people to great and mighty achievements are its artists and strategists, philosophers and politicians, men thrown up by destiny and providence. Rudolf Hess, my assistant of many years standing, would tell you: If we have such a leader, God is with us.[31]

'We wish to spare our people bloody wars and destruction. For this reason I regard the spirit of self-sacrifice as the highest virtue, not only in wartime but also in the political battle. Naturally I do not mean self-sacrifice in lost battles or hopeless parliamentary struggles. The war will be won by the study of Clausewitz and Schlieffen, in Krupp's workshops, in the Rhineland mines and round the green baize tables of the Reich Chancellery in the Wilhelmstrasse. What does the Day of National Mourning mean today? Floods of tears for the fallen. Are we to remain pacifist for ever and live for ever under the Treaty of Versailles? The British pay homage to Shakespeare and swear on the Bible, but they keep battleships to rule the seas. Their hypocrisy should be unmasked before our people. Similarly the lies about the rights of man, the legacy of the French Revolution, must be exposed. We have no wish to live on Church charity. As Chamberlain said after 1918, we have to choose whether we wish to be the hammer or the anvil, whether we would prefer to strike or be struck. Anyone who decides to belong to the hammers, to the strikers, is a hero. Equally the man who goes out on to the street and sets the German people on the move is as much of a hero as the soldier who fell on the Somme or at the Masurian Lakes. The time will come when the Day of National Mourning will be a day of remembrance not only for those who fell in the war but also for those who have sacrificed themselves for the movement.[32] We cannot recapture our political power without our movement and without a reawakening in Germany; without that we cannot bring the Germanic peoples together or secure our people's *lebensraum*. This political struggle is no ordinary party political agitation; it concerns the creative genius of our race. Either we can do it in ten years and then war will be over for all time and I shall devote myself to building; alternatively for a thousand years to come we must expend our sweat on the forging of guns.[33] Of course in my ripe old age, between sixty and seventy, I would like to devote myself to architecture. In view of our intellect and technical resources we Germans have something to contribute in this field. As I have already explained to you, we are interested neither in a civil war nor in a military showdown with our neighbours.'

(Suddenly Hitler flies into a rage)

'Eventually, however, the policeman at home in the shape

of the German conservatives and the international policeman in the shape of British and French plutocracy must shake themselves free of their string-pullers. You know as well as I do that when they agitate against us they do so because behind them stands the Jew. They want to fish in troubled waters. Eventually we must solve this problem. By that time we must be so strong that no one will be able to foment revolution among us and no one will even think of opposing a people which is demanding its *lebensraum.*[34] If this is to happen, world plutocracy must distinguish between the empty words of our present-day politicians and the effective action of a government prepared for the greatest sacrifices. This government, however, must be backed by a reawakened people. Our demands must be backed by force and boldness of decision. Should the anti-German forces then stir up unrest against us and initiate an encirclement policy in order to keep the children of Versailles and Locarno in poverty, then the guns must bark. In this event their road to Canossa will be even more humiliating. There is no better soldier in the world than the German; the gentlemen in Paris and London know that. Or do you think differently, Herr Breiting?'

(Hitler spoke as incisively as if he possessed the greatest army in the world. Any incautious remark on my part could have brought the conversation to an end)

BREITING: 'Our greatest wish is to avoid civil wars or wars with foreign enemies.'

HITLER: 'I wish to conceal nothing from you. You should now know that we regard events from an historical standpoint. I am speaking so frankly because I am convinced that in your heart there is some echo of my feelings. If you are not to know our plan for the reorganisation of Europe, who is to?

'Well then, I demand the return of Austria to the Reich and also the incorporation of the German-speaking areas of Bohemia, the Sudetenland. The Austrian Anschluss will present no difficulty. I wonder, however, what attitude German-speaking Switzerland will adopt to this problem. You know as well as I do that Zurich, Basle and Berne are German cities. From what one reads in the *Neue Zürcher Zeitung* and the Basle newspapers there will only be a temporary period of separatism. Tessin, as we know, is Italian speaking and the mere name Lugano shows where that belongs. The French could have Geneva and Lausanne as compensation for their other losses. Belgium is a mere artificial monstrosity of a state where monarchy and Church are trying to hold the balance between Flemings and Walloons. The Flemings speak the same language as the Dutch and only the monarchy and the Church are holding these two germanic countries apart. We have never written off Alsace and Lorraine; Dijon was a Burgundian city and Lyons was the starting point for the southward march of the Goths. We cannot stop Nice, Corsica and the Italian alpine areas going to our ally. If the French challenge us, there should be Basque, Breton and Burgundian States in France.[35] What goes for the West goes also for the East and South-east. For a thousand years Austria imposed her culture on the Danube basin and the South-east. The fate of Vienna in 1918 was due solely to the spinelessness of the Habsburg monarchy. The only people to attempt to follow the road of germanism were one Emperor, Joseph II, one Chancellor, Bach (1852-1859), and a few great racial thinkers such as Schönerer.[36] We shall send our knights forth upon their trail.[37] Catholicism may, however, put a spoke in our wheel. Hungary will be a natural ally since she was dismembered by the Treaty of Versailles just like Germany. One and a half million Hungarians live outside their country's frontiers. Siebenburg and the greater part of the Voivodina are Hungarian territories. 250,000 Germans live in Siebenburg. Moreover we shall not forget the strong German minority at the mouth of the Danube and Save; we shall demand their regrouping and resettlement. Belgrade was, and still is,

Prince Eugen's fortress. Croatia, like Slovakia, will also be an independent state if the Serbs and Bohemians do not come to their senses. Bratislava and Zagreb are mere suburbs of Vienna. The people there must learn to speak German again and so acquire German respectability. We intend to renounce the ex-Austrian areas of Trieste and Istria. Dalmatia and the Balkan areas beyond will be placed under Italian influence. We have no doubt that our future ally will open the ports of Trieste and Fiume to our shipping. The nearest ally in the South-east will be Bulgaria. Macedonia is Bulgarian territory. Bulgaria must have an outlet to the Aegean. In short, Austria, Switzerland, Belgium, Yugoslavia and Czechoslovakia must disappear as states; Poland and Rumania must change their status. Both these two countries are a biological reservoir of Jewry. Of the ten million Jews in Europe half live in these countries. Mannerheim and Finland know what to expect from the Bolshevists sooner or later. King Boris was always a friend of Germany and will remain so in future. I intend to allot a special mission to Finland and Bulgaria. We propose to build a protective wall against Russian imperialism and the Slavs from Northern Norway to the Black Sea, for we must not forget that Stalin's communism is a new form of Russian imperialism. Even during the War Hindenburg referred to the "Russian menace" when Sven Hedin visited him in his headquarters. Stalin is no more than a Russian imperialist, a successor to Ivan the Terrible, as a Vienna professor said to me recently. No German, whether he belongs to my party or not, can evade this determination to establish a new order. This is not a question of Adolf Hitler but of the abolition of the Versailles *diktat* and the establishment of a new order in Europe. What do you think about it?'

BREITING: 'To be honest, Herr Hitler, my fear is that England and France will never approve such a disturbance of the European balance. Such a policy will also be opposed by the Catholic Church which exercises great influence in various countries in the Danube basin and in the West. Our correspondents in Brussels, Vienna, Rome and even Budapest report that Rosenberg's book *Der Mythus des 20 Jahrhunderts* has caused great disquiet in the Vatican and in Catholic circles in various countries. In addition non-Catholic circles in the South-east have close ties with England and France. Similarly Italy is keenly interested in the fate of Austria.'

HITLER: 'I know that what you tell me is what your correspondents report to you. These gentlemen have good reason to report in this way. They know that, if we win, we shall have no further need of them for our continental information network. At present they are still free to throw dust in the eyes of our people with their pessimism. What does the European balance of power mean, now in 1931? Lloyd George, Baldwin and Macdonald could think this way in 1918 but thirteen years have gone by since then; England has problems to solve in India, Africa, the Middle East and the Far East. But we have no wish to drive England from her present positions of power. In an age of nationalism and anti-colonialism with the economic crisis increasing all the time the British Empire cannot continue without our support. What your correspondents report is one thing; what my experts like Professor Haushofer forecast is another. A large number of intelligent and influential Englishmen welcome the reorganisation of Europe and Germany.'[38]

(Hess, listening calmly, nods his agreement)

'My experts are studying these problems in a strictly scientific manner taking account of the geopolitical, economic, ethnic and strategic factors. Your correspondents, on the other hand, merely report the suggestions of certain circles in Paris, Zurich, Vienna or New York. They run with the hare and hunt with the hounds. We have no intention of destroying the British Empire. We have no objection to His Majesty's flag flying over Suez, Singapore and Hong Kong. Let no one think that we are jealous of England's overseas power. On the contrary, I have always maintained that we have a natural ally and that that is England. But we do not propose to support England if she opposes our reconstruction and prevents us exercising our rights on the continent. In America the City Bank and its accomplices must know that, with the revival of Japan, they are sitting on a powder barrel in the Far East. And what of China? I do not want to go into that. I merely say that we are in a favourable world situation. For this reason we want power, not simply in order to rule, but to pursue a world policy. We have no intention of hoisting the swastika flag on Buckingham Palace or Windsor Castle; we wish to preserve the colonial world. The French too should keep the Cameroons, Syria and North Africa. But Messrs Herriot, Blum and Mandel must not have the temerity to intrigue against our growing Reich. If they do, we shall not respect their possessions in the colonial world. The Arabs are merely waiting for some disturbance. The French bourgeoisie and military will have to choose – either Herriot-Blum and continuation of the encirclement policy now being pursued against Germany, or renunciation of all that and assumption of a fitting role in Western Europe.[39] England and France must come to some agreement with Italy about the position in the Mediterranean and clarify the continental situation with us. As soon as we assume power we shall launch the idea of a Four-Power Pact for the reorganisation of Europe and this must receive approval from Paris and London.[40] The British will not give up their holiday bungalows or their sailing and rowing regattas for the sake of the Soviet Union. We need raw materials and we can now get them from France and England. Trade will develop and we shall select the banks and firms with which we wish to do business. We can therefore offer opportunities for export. At the moment we have no need to build a high seas fleet. We will give England and France every assurance in this respect. Once we have secured our *lebensraum* in Europe, then we can demand our equality of status on the seas. Admirals Lützow and Trotha were right when they said that mastery of the seas was an industrial problem. At present we have no need to build a great fleet, but we must have a modern air force. Göring and his friends have first-class ideas on how to get civil aviation and the air defence of the Reich going. Moreover the youth of England will look to the new Germany as an example. We shall have modern armed forces and that in a few years time. Not even the Channel is a valid line of defence today, so how should the French Generals' defences be one? Your correspondents may report about the balance of power, but this balance depends upon the military force possessed by various powers on the continent of Europe. We shall have new weapons and the best soldiers. Joffre did not win the victory of the Marne nor Foch that of Verdun; our senior commanders were incompetent and incapable of appreciating the advantages of the brilliant Schlieffen Plan.[41] The Generals at the front regarded their armies as their own property. In addition, from 1914 to 1918 our men had to fight on two fronts. The officers are right nowadays to celebrate Schlieffen's birthday, for now they know where they made the mistakes. All this is a problem of encirclement battles as Schlieffen demonstrated in his *Cannae*. I have studied this plan with some officers. It is really unique. In two years' time we shall be celebrating the centenary of Schlieffen's birth and then we will speak our mind on the subject.[42] Kaiser William thought like an Englishman. He wanted to conduct an oceanic policy from continental Germany. He dreamt of a great fleet and colonial empires all at the same time and allowed himself to become involved in war both in East and West. In addition he allowed the bravery of our soldiers to be cancelled out by the enemy's superiority in equipment and by political fraud. If British tanks and American artillery had not arrived and if we had been able to employ in the West the divisions tied down in Russia, Foch would not have dictated the armistice to us in Compiègne; we should have dictated it to him in Versailles. Field Marshal Ludendorff has assured me of this many times. We have learnt much from the First World War and in future we shall continue to draw our conclusions from it.'

(Hitler's temper rises and he speaks most emphatically)

'If, despite our justifiable action, armed conflicts ensue because world Jewry would like to turn back the wheel of history, Jewry will be crushed by that same wheel. I do not believe, however, in the possibility of war since, if the Jews can first be excluded from economic and political life in Germany, they will no longer be able to find partners abroad.[43] Göring was here a few days ago and brought with him certain people from the aircraft industry. He told me that, should it ever come to this, one or two of our bomber squadrons over London would be enough to cause the British to hoist the white flag on the Houses of Parliament. The same goes for Paris of course. Whether it be Churchill or Blum, both will be strung up by their own people for betrayal of peace and understanding between nations – like Louis XVI in his time. But it will not come to that, for this time the British will find no friends on the continent. Never shall a British soldier set foot on German soil. The French will be careful not to become involved in such adventures. Sweden, Norway, Finland, Denmark, Holland and Belgium will not be party to the French or Franco-Saxon encirclement game; they will not even remain neutral; they will agree with us. Our technical and scientific presence will be as welcome in Stockholm, Copenhagen or Amsterdam as in Vienna or Zurich and Strasbourg.'

(Hitler fixes me with a compelling eye and gives the impression that he is referring, not to some dream, but to reality)

'Not even Poland, Czechoslovakia or Yugoslavia will have any different view of the situation. What do you think of Lord Beaverbrook and his mammoth newspaper, the *Daily Telegraph* (*sic*)? Do you think that he will understand our position? To judge by the way he is campaigning for a new order in the Danube area, he will support a new order for Europe as a whole.'

BREITING: 'I admire your optimism, Herr Hitler.'

HITLER: 'I have already had that said to me by other people to whom I have spoken exactly as I have to you. Officers and industrialists are far more confident than intellectuals, I can assure you. Naturally we have much work still to do. But it is the duty of our professors, publicists and journalists to present both these facts and the long-term views of the thinking section of our people in a correct light, instead of talking about the obsolete balance of power in Europe or adventurism and spreading horror stories about foreign intervention. Look at the confidence with which the Italian intelligentsia follows the Duce. Why? They know that Benito Mussolini is constructing a colossal empire which will put the Roman Empire in the shade. We shall put up a memorial to Mussolini in every city. Italy will be eternally grateful to him for his victories. Mussolini is a typical representative of our alpine race which, in everything it does, has its eye on eternity.

'Just think how well the British journalists and press magnates write in support of their imperial interests. The London *Times* has become a national institution. Over there people cannot write such nonsense about the British as you will find written about the Germans in our major newspapers. Why should something which is a matter of course in England, not be possible in Germany? No one says a word over there when the Chamberlain family amasses a fortune through the wars in South Africa and India. Churchill, the bankrupt of Gallipoli, still has political ambitions. Here we spend our time cursing the industrialists and arms merchants. We must reach agreement with the Spanish, Hungarian and Bulgarian officer corps and with nationalists in various European countries, more particularly with Mussolini's Italy. We need have no fear of foreign intervention against a reawakened Germany. The strong are never attacked, only the weak. Our first steps will be to offer our hand to England and France. We will establish friendly relations with their businessmen, military, publicists and scientists. We do not intend to tilt at windmills like Cervantes' hero. Though I come of a lowly background, I can speak several types of language. What I mean, and I repeat, is that we shall not behave like a bull in a china shop. We also intend to set up a great intelligence service and in doing so we shall have in mind the places where our enemies find that the shoe pinches.[44] England and France owe much to their secret services. If we are to pursue a power policy, we must not be pusillanimous; with fanatical determination we must have faith in our victory and must know everything that goes on in the enemy camp. Discouragement and fear psychosis stem solely from the traitor press. Construction of a great German cultural and economic community – what a programme and what a healthy role for our press. Three months ago, in February 1931, Germany's delegate Schacht was negotiating about the Young Plan. I tell you we do not need the 500-million dollar aid. Foreign aid from the United States destroys our reputation. If, through their secret service, the French hatch some plot with Schleicher against me, we shall discredit these officers in the eyes of the people and pillory other countries for interfering in our internal affairs.[45] Sooner or later officers who do this sort of thing will be branded as traitors and dealt with. I have no intention of bringing down President Hindenburg, but naturally I shall stand as a candidate at the next Presidential election in order to show him that he will be elected by 30-40 per cent marxist votes against 30-40 per cent nationalist.[46]

'There will then be many changes among the nationalists. In Thuringia, Brunswick and Oldenburg the Nationalists are not averse to co-operation with the National-Socialists. There will shortly be a meeting between people from the Stahlhelm and the Landbund, representatives of the Reichswehr and of finance such as Schacht, to find some common basis for reconstruction.[47] We do not forget the influence of the churches. There will definitely be no Vatican crusade against us. We know Monsignor Pacelli since he was the Vatican's diplomatic representative in Germany for twelve years; as Secretary of State and adviser to Pope Pius XI it is greatly in his interest that the German Catholics should at last have a statute. People like von Papen and many others in Munich are already at work and are establishing good relations with the Vatican.[48] And that despite Rosenberg's bogey book. That book contains much that is true, but it is not timely. It is not intended for the masses; it is rather ideological education for the intelligentsia.[49] Many books have been banned by the Vatican but it has not therefore conducted a crusade against the countries in which those books were written or printed. After all what are 100,000 copies of a book compared to a Concordat making religious education obligatory in the schools. Pacelli saw the Red republic in Munich; so have no fear: there will be no second *kulturkampf* in Germany. There will be no discontent in our country, for we shall be a nation once more. Religious strife, party struggles and electoral campaigns are merely attempts to divide and degrade our nation, as the Weimar system has amply proved. An end will be put to these practices. The USA has become a state as a result of liberalist ideas and various other factors, through financial monopolies too. But they will never be a nation; they will always be the scene of internal disturbances, ideological, religious, ethnic and racial rivalries. For the people now in power in America a unified Germany is a strange idea. Anyway, they are a long way off geographically and we can do much to assist them to remain in isolation. On the day when we schedule our showdown with the Soviet Union the isolationist forces in America will be on our side. America can keep her system, but she will never be able to dictate to us our historic path. The USA will be overtaken by events. But we cannot stand idly by and watch what is taking place in Russia, for that is happening on our own continent. The most dangerous force in the world is Russian imperialism, Slav imperialism in combination with the dictatorship of the proletariat. If that symbiosis should come to pass ... Think of the reservoir of manpower and raw material resources at Stalin's disposal!

'Our publicity men should already be thumping the drum today. The menace to western civilisation was never so great. Even before we assume power we must make clear to the British, French and Americans and the Vatican too that sooner or later we shall be forced to conduct a crusade against bolshevism. England and France should be grateful to us for having recognised the danger in time. What does it matter to them who rules in Russia tomorrow? We must already be thinking of the resettlement of millions of men from Germany and Europe.[50] Migrations of peoples have always taken place. In the single year 1641 (*sic*) 50,000 Irishmen left for North America and two-thirds of the country remained uninhabited. What a lot of nordic blood has flowed to the United States. We must colonise the East ruthlessly. Moreover we must not forget the world distribution of raw materials. Look at what is happening in Latin America. I have to thank my friend Ernst Röhm, the Chief of Staff,[51] for the fact that I am well informed about conditions in Bolivia; he was a military instructor there. The country is rich in lead, copper, zinc, wolfram and gold. Nevertheless it lacks iron and coal. England and America may dominate world trade today but our trading capacity will change once we rule the eastern area. We think of a white South Africa, a white Australia and New Zealand, but we cannot countenance anything but a white Ukraine and a white Caucasus. How should the Portuguese and Spaniards continue to colonise Africa and South America when their resources are so small because they have no home industries. We would be glad to help them. Our prestige in South America is great. Many of Röhm's letters told me so. Unfortunately the sources of raw materials there are in the hands of Anglo-Saxon plutocracy and it is acting unreasonably. Think of the turn-over of Royal Dutch Shell, Anglo-Iranian Oil or Katanga Union and then compare our geographical possibilities in the East.[52] The Middle East is not far off either. One of the Hohenzollerns launched the idea of the Berlin-Baghdad railway and people like von Papen fought for it in Palestine. Are we really to remain a nation of have-nots for ever? Why should not the sources of raw materials be equitably distributed? We have the capacity to rouse and lead the masses against this situation. In the long term ought Germany to be ground down economically? Everywhere there is discontent. Everywhere people are awaiting a new world order. We intend to introduce a great resettlement policy; we do not wish to go on treading on each other's toes in Germany. In 1923 little Greece could resettle a million men. Think of the biblical deportations and the massacres of the Middle Ages (Rosenberg refers to them) and remember the extermination of the Armenians. One eventually reaches the conclusion that masses of men are mere biological plasticine. We will not allow ourselves to be turned into niggers as the French tried to do after 1918. The nordic blood available in England, northern France and North America will eventually go with us to reorganise the world. The discontent in their own home countries and in their colonies will leave them no choice.'

BREITING: 'I do not doubt, Herr Hitler, that there is great discontent in some countries. But everybody is not happy in Germany either. How should we avoid further internal conflicts?'

HITLER: 'Quite simply: follow the NSDAP which points the way to the only solution. We have found a solution to every problem – the unemployed, agriculture, culture or defence. And should there be a famine, then we must solve the problem from our own resources by rationalisation. Our soil produces only 25 per cent of our requirements. With a little goodwill and intelligent rationalisation we could cover 50 per cent or even 75 per cent of our needs; but how can this happen if our land is mortgaged, our machines idle and our men unemployed? Do not forget that six million acres of fruitful soil are labouring under a 100 per cent mortgage. Now, we can solve that – by a distribution of duties within industry and agriculture. We must use radical methods.'

BREITING: 'I understand your preoccupations, but are you not taking upon yourself insoluble problems which your opponents will use to their own advantage?'

HITLER: 'I tell you for the hundredth time: One cannot build a house without first levelling the ground and laying the foundations. We must give reawakened Germany a programme which will appeal both to the heart and to the mind. It is this long-range programme, Germany's role on the continent, which will be more inspiring to the soul of the people, the intelligentsia and the officers than all so-called social legislation and economic planning. First we must become masters in our own house and then we can plant our garden with corn and vegetables. We no longer intend to be drawers of water and shedders of blood for other people.

'I tell you, Herr Breiting, Germany will awake more quickly than many pessimistic intellectuals imagine. People will stream along to us from all sides; our membership lists will soon be filled. In fact we are interested, not in quantity, but in quality. Only decent people will be employed in the new Germany, so that we shall never have to fear another 1918 stab in the back.'

BREITING: 'But the armistice was imposed on us not solely by the stab in the back. As early as September 1918 our commanders, Hindenburg and Ludendorff, had demanded an armistice.'

HITLER: I have discussed these questions in detail with Ludendorff. His reason for demanding an armistice in the autumn of 1918 was not that he regarded our armies as beaten but because we lacked all political leadership. The workers and soldiers back behind were about to mutiny. Think of the munitions strike. Clemenceau had deserters and pacifists shot. On our side the protagonists of the idea of holding on were held up to ridicule. I repeat to you – had there been a decent political leader at the head of the Reich, the last battalion in the field would definitely have been German. And then this collapse would never have happened. The political situation in Germany at the present moment is similar to that of 1917/18. Germany is led, not by Germans, but by international parasites. They have no wish to see a strong Germany; their masters in Paris, London and New York would not allow it. We shall see our so-called German politicians – hounded on from abroad – trying to ban our party. But neither Braun nor Severing would be capable of that – nor Grzesinski![53] The creatures, the grave-diggers in this Reich, are numerous. They have taken the republic under their wing and therefore it must go under. The ship will sink with all hands. They are using every method to maintain their position, particularly in Prussia which constitutes two-thirds of Germany. They tell me that I am an Austrian and have no business here. They are protagonists of federalism and separatism. But we would rather die as Prussian unifiers than Bavarian or Austrian separatists.[54] On the day when we are entrusted with the business of government – and that on the basis of a decree from the Reich President – I will put the spoilers out of business and draw the overwhelming majority of the people to us. One of our first decisions should be to ban the communist party.[55] The majority of the Social Democrats can be re-educated. The majority of officials think only of their job and their pension. Every German will be at liberty to exercise his judgement on historic events. We wish to rule with the backing of the overwhelming majority of the people. A year after our assumption of power the notions of parliamentarianism and federalism will have been expunged from our constitution. Whether the parasites like it or not, the German people will decide that for once there shall be a non-Prussian Chancellor in Prussia. And then the Prussian military virtues will be a shining light for the entire people. The present system's politicians sit up there, not to obey the will of the people, but to keep our country in a state of impotence under cover of federalism and parliamentarianism. The higher an enemy can rise in the hierarchy of the state, the greater the damage he can do to the Reich. For this reason I say that these criminals in high places are far more poisonous than the little gangs of toughs. We shall stamp on the serpent's head, not its tail. The financial hyenas are screaming their heads off because they know that we shall never founder in a morass of opportunism. They put on a show and spread around music-hall jokes about us; they try to mislead people with atrocity stories. If only these small-timers at least had some imagination! But simply because they rule the cultural institutions and the press, they can get their publicity cheap. One day they will let the red hordes loose upon us. But there will never be a red republic period again; the spirit of Potsdam and Königsberg will win the day.[56] Germany can only achieve political power through the German military virtues. Pacifism, cosmopolitanism, federalism and parliamentarianism must be ruthlessly exterminated. We require a unified national territory. All the *Länder* must have the same laws and be directed by one central government.[57] Without this as a basis we cannot achieve our politico-military aims.'

BREITING: 'Herr Hitler, I do not think that I am asking a treasonable question if I enquire concerning the NSDAP's views on defence policy and national defence.'

HITLER: 'This question too I can answer frankly. It is understood of course that this point will remain a matter between us. Why should you not know what many of our Reichswehr officers know already? We do not, however, wish to be labelled as revanchists by the marxists. That would be inexpedient politically. One thing is certain, however: our rearmament will begin on the day we assume power.

Germany's enemies will attempt to form a front against us both at home and abroad. We shall have to act quickly but intelligently. In the first place we must strike down our internal enemy. Goebbels has always taken the word "attack" as the basis for our action.[58] Offence is always the best defence. The political awakening must go hand in hand with an effort towards real national defence. On this I am agreed with those officers who support our cause. I served for five full years in the German army. I had no wish to make it my career; I just did my duty like anyone else. When the war ended I realised that we had no lack of good commanders; what we lacked were decent politicians. It was for this reason that I took the decision to become a politician. The Reichswehr has always given proof of its respectability. In November 1923 we were shot at, not by the Reichswehr, but by the green-uniformed police. The reorganisation of the Reichswehr will create no great difficulties. It will be far harder work to reorganise the administrative machine and the police who have been under marxist pressure for years. With their 100,000 soldiers officers like Rundstedt, Reichenau, Beck, Blomberg and Fritsch are to all intents and purposes powerless today. With its mere 45 regiments what can this Reichswehr do against the internal and external enemy?[59] Among our political and criminal police officers there are undoubtedly vigorous anti-communists to be found. But few police officers think on *völkisch* and historic lines. The situation in the police is quite different from that in the Reichswehr. Police officers who are anti-communist are merely obeying the call of the Social Democrats. It is the old struggle for votes. Only a few senior police officials have spotted the Jewish woodworm. Only an anti-semite is a true anti-communist. It is only thanks to the alertness of these few political and criminal police officials that we have been able to avoid many an attack. Our friends know that the communists are in the service solely of Jewish plutocracy. A Jew who calls himself a communist is, after all, still a Jew.

The Jewish problem is a highly complex matter. I do not wish to go into that today. You know, however, that our ideology is opposed to the interests of the Chosen Race and that we abominate their dance around the Golden Calf. For racial and financial reasons the Jews are basically opposed to communism.'

BREITING: 'And Marx? Marx was, after all, a Jew.'

HITLER: 'This question carries us too far. It is easy to see why Marx formulated the idea of class warfare. Abraham and Moses, protestantism and catholicism were insufficient to woo the workers away from their love of country. We have already discussed the failure of the bourgeoisie in its leadership role and its incapacity to win the proletariat over to the popular community. It is due to Marx that we can no longer recapture the proletariat by words alone. It will not even be enough simply to solve their social problems. We shall find ourselves forced to use administrative methods. I understand very well what the separation of powers means. That may be acceptable in England. For us the supreme law of the constitution is: whatever serves the vital interests of the nation is legal. We intend to recapture the politically-minded masses by this method. The internal and international criminal gang will either be forced to work or simply exterminated. We need new policies in administration, education and health. Our party comrade Frank always thinks that everything can be settled in the law courts. We have other lawyers, however, who say that a policeman can be a judge or a judge a policeman. We have no time for paper warfare or moralist discussions before deciding how the criminal element should be dealt with. I wish to give officials greater discretion. The State's authority will be increased thereby. I wish to transform the non-political criminal police into a political instrument of the highest State authority. Manual labour never did anyone any harm and we shall set up great labour camps for all forms of parasite. The Spaniards started the idea in Cuba and the British in South Africa. Even today we must calculate how we can best render innocuous those who try to incite people to internal unrest and general strikes.[60] We demand that functionally the Party agencies dovetail into the various authorities of the administration. In Italy fascism has produced a masterly solution to this problem. I do not wish to ape my friend Mussolini. We are not a monarchy and we have no Pope in the country. We are a far greater industrial power than Italy. Our internal enemies are far more active than those in Italy. Our economic problems differ from those of our southern neighbour. Our rise to power has no prospects of success unless we place our physical and mental energies at the service of total mobilisation. The adverse ratio between our armaments and those of our enemies cannot be eliminated so long as we, a nation of 70 million, have an army no larger than the Belgians with their 7 million inhabitants. Without National-Socialist leadership of the State we cannot achieve effective national defence. With the situation as it is today Poland could move into East Prussia any day. This would not cause the Russians and French to declare war on Poland. How can we defend our frontiers in all directions with 4,000 officers which is all the Treaty of Versailles allows us? Our infantry regiments are limited to 76 officers and 2,450 men, cavalry regiments to 30 officers and 700 troopers,[61] to say nothing of machine guns and field howitzers. That is only adequate for street fighting. Are we to play at undercover soldiers for ever? Frontier protection service, Black Reichswehr, Defence Associations, Carrier Pigeon Associations, rifle-shooting and sports associations! All chicken feed. This underground business is unworthy of our people. Agreed, we had our experiences with the Free Corps. Noske, the Social Democrat, made use of them to suppress the Spartacist movement. Once that was done, the black man had served his purpose and could go. Even today Reichswehr headquarters counts upon the SA, SS, Stahlhelm and Youth Sports League for national defence. But what is that compared to the 350,000 or 400,000 strapping recruits whom we could train each year by introducing universal national service. Article 177 of the Versailles Treaty even forbids us to introduce defence exercises for students and athletes. These associations such as the SA and SS are a revolutionary force and the Party's emergency defence force, but our glorious undefeated army will always remain the real bearer of arms. The party militia and barrack police can be used against the internal enemy, but the army is not fitted for that.'[62]

BREITING: 'Recently, however, we saw disturbances break out in your own organisation and they were a source of jubilation to your opponents.'

HITLER: 'Disturbances is too strong a word. Our enemies are trying to infiltrate themselves everywhere. Stennes, the SA Commander in Berlin, permitted a *putsch* to be instigated against me.[63] My SS obeyed my orders loyally and honestly and only individual SA commanders adhered to Stennes. The rank and file turned away from the troublemakers.[64] It is quite possible that we shall have such people on our hands once more. A revolution cannot proceed without internal difficulties. There are so many opportunists trying to swim with the tide. My information service has already reported to me that my enemies are speculating upon the possibility that these internal difficulties might force me to give up. Never shall I give up my programme and my aim. I have always said that people were trying to split my party. They have offered money to the Gruppenführer and Gauleiter. People want to try to split us and dupe us. But these expatriates will never succeed with their dirty business. We are already in process of taking additional protective measures. We know all the poisoners' recipes. Soon we shall have our own intelligence service and it will be more effective than the political and criminal police of our Social Democrat rulers. I intend to construct a highly skilled headquarters to protect the people and the State. It will be a secret service which will bring to nought the plans of the

French Deuxième Bureau and the British Secret Service. Our political intelligence will put the Cheka in the shade.[65] This is possible for us because we tolerate no infiltration in our ranks. But there can be no revival so long as a traitorous opposition exists in our country. Kaiser William II offered the Social Democrat leaders his hand in reconciliation. Even while shaking the imperial hand, they were reaching for their dagger with the other.[66] For the internal enemy there is only the savage alternative – either-or. The Jew will have no choice but to get out of Germany and Europe in good time. Even the Arabs do not want the Jews. Why should we tolerate them here? They will be expelled, not by me but by the German people. It may even be that they will come to me for protection. This is no question of ideology but of genuine national feeling. I have already told you that I do not intend to massacre the Jews. Perhaps, however, they should be thinking of emigration even now. What does the bourgeoisie think of the Jewish problem, Herr Breiting? I know that it is a thorny question.'

BREITING: 'Herr Hitler, I do not want to be misunderstood. There are both good and bad people among the Jews. Many gave their lives for their country in the last war. Many wear the Iron Cross. I know many who are bitterly anti-communist. There are Jews who would wish to talk to you quite differently.'

HITLER: 'They are few and far between, however.'

BREITING: 'They are rarities because they receive such bad treatment from your propagandists. There are able and capable men among them. Think of Einstein, after all.'

HITLER: 'Everything they have produced has been stolen from us. All their knowledge they use against us. Let them go and create unrest among other peoples. We do not need them. We can do nothing with them.[67] I have said many times that propaganda is not a scientific argument but has its roots in national sentiment. The germanic sentiment is now aflame and the masses are marching under the swastika banner. We do not work with unorganised mobs. The fanatical flood of our people has its goal and it will be directed down broad highways, as Schiller said of the bronze which flowed fully formed from the cast. At the far end of our highway we shall be holding our flag high. This is our march route and it will be directed by our organisation and our propaganda. The party organisation is already at work selecting members from this flood. We organise them in various groups – Youth, workers, peasants, self-employed, industry, SA, SS, police. We are no amorphous mass; we wish to take possession of the entire people.[68] As you will understand, such an organisation can tolerate no foreign bodies and we are obligated to take our defensive measures in good time. I tell you quite frankly that you would not be sitting before me here today had I not information which testifies to the soundness of your attitude and background.[69] A statesman and propaganda genius is not merely someone who dispenses the written word; he also knows how to choose his friends and associates. The effectiveness of propaganda rises and falls with the capacity to produce ideas. The strength of an idea is seen in its fulfilment. We have constructed a machine and within this machine we shall form special bodies in which many men, who now hold aloof, will be able to demonstrate their capabilities. We need competent collaborators in the defence forces, in the economy and in the cultural and journalistic world. That does not imply, however, that we shall censure or take revenge on people who think differently. No state can be formed with blockheads. The bolsheviks destroyed their intelligentsia and expelled the Russian captains of industry, and they cannot recover from that. I put my trust in a coalition of the NSDAP, the German Nationalists and the sound elements of the Peoples Party. We have a long way to go together. Give my best wishes to Herr Hugenberg and Herr Oberfohren. My best wishes too to Herr Herfurth. Tell them all that Germany can never return to her strength without National-Socialism.'[70]

*   *   *

The conversation ended at 12.45 p.m. and Hitler was even more brisk than when we had assembled at 10.0. I had the impression that he would gladly have kept me to lunch. Hess told me, however, that a mass of files was waiting to be dealt with. I asked Hess whether perhaps my questions had irritated Hitler. 'Why should they?' Hess asked. 'You are not a party member after all. It all went off very well.' Hess asked me to send him a transcript of my shorthand notes. He impressed on me the necessity of respecting Hitler's frankness and keeping the contents of the discussion to myself.

B R E I T I N G ' S comments on his second meeting with Hitler:

So speaks Hitler. He has a good memory; he juggles with ideas; his character is incomprehensible to me. For two hours he spoke without notes about his doctrine and his 'scientific' method of dealing with the internal enemy, quoting economic statistics and historical dates. Nevertheless he definitely did not tell me all. What I learnt today is a complete mystery to me. I am now convinced that, should he come to power, he will persecute the Jews. His tirades of hate against the Jews were no mere intimidation manoeuvre. He has no wish to hang them from the telegraph poles, as he said at the first meeting, but he will compel them to emigrate. Even Albert Einstein is a foreigner to him. What crazy ideas these are! I have the impression that he has no fear of the communists. His anti-communism is merely the common denominator to which he wishes to bring the other parties, the churches, the Reichswehr and the bourgeoisie. Undoubtedly he will have a showdown with communism. His crusade against the Soviet Union is merely the excuse for rearmament. God preserve us from this 'architect' and 'liberator'.

He regards the best of our bourgeoisie as a cesspit full of thieves. He wants to submerge and crush everything like a tidal wave. And he wants to have done all this by his fifty-second birthday. In two years' time, therefore, he wishes to face the bourgeoisie, the Reichswehr and the churches with the alternative: Soviet Germany or a National-Socialist Reich.

At our first meeting I was struck by his chin, which seemed to wish to crush everything. This time I observed his jackboots which seemed to want to trample on everything. He hopes that industry, the Reichswehr and Hindenburg will help him. The first thing he wants to do is to grind down the communists. And in the service of that cause the bourgeoisie should go to Canossa.

His ideas on the new order in Germany and Europe seem to me utopian. I hope, nevertheless, that during the next two years political realities will compel him to adopt a new language. Hugenberg said to me: 'Like a trader he puts his price high at first so as to be able to give something away later.' My only lasting hope is that men like Hindenburg, von Papen and Hugenberg will be able to bring him to reason. Oberfohren thinks that, if he insists on his extreme views, he will land in Landsberg for a second spell. Schleicher and the Generals will never allow him to set up a dictatorship.[71]

I suspect that the brown-shirted dictator speaks on these lines, not only to me, but to anyone whom he wishes to turn into a friend. His words show that he finds a profitable and receptive audience among officers and industrialists. Now I understand also why these people talk about his hypnotic eyes. It seems to me that many people like listening to this megalomania. National-Socialist Fata Morgana! If one day our officers, industrialists and intellectuals actually approve this programme, then we are heading for catastrophe. Now I know what the totality of his idealogy means. I may neither write nor speak about it; I have given my word and I shall keep it. I think, however, that I shall be betraying nothing if I give Herr Herfurth a short report and speak privately to Hugenberg and Oberfohren.

EPILOGUE

by Dr. Edouard Calic

The Anatomy of Demagogy and Adolf Hitler's Bent for Destruction

In his talks with Richard Breiting Hitler revealed his plans and intentions in a way which, for good reason, he never did in speeches intended for the people. Breiting hardly spoke and was extremely cautious in giving vent to his misgivings. As his final comment shows, however, what he had heard finally left him profoundly uneasy.

His wife, Emmy Breiting, assured me that she can clearly remember her husband returning from the second interview and saying to her: 'If Hitler comes to power, he will be the end of us all.' For several days he mulled over what Hitler had said.

Breiting felt himself under an obligation to keep his word to Hitler not to publish details of these talks in the press. His papers, however, show clearly that he warned Dingeldey, the leader of his party at the time, together with Hugenberg and Oberfohren, the most influential members of the German Nationalists; he also allowed them to see partial transcripts of his shorthand notes, as he did Herfurth, Goerdeler and Bünger. The question remains: what political combinations were at work to bring the conservative right wing ultimately to make a pact with Hitler despite such warnings and misgivings? What are the underlying reasons which caused Hitler's sophisticated scheming to succeed?

We hear today of Hitler's capabilities, not only as a demagogue, but as a 'demon', convincing individuals and casting a spell over the masses. To this metaphysical argument is added an equally irrational theme: in a situation of great stress and through a chain of fatal circumstances the German people had the misfortune to turn this man into a dictator. Such statements were merely an attempt to banish the real reasons for the catastrophe into which the German people was plunged. They were countered by a further speculative idea – that Hitler was politically incompetent, sick, obsessed by chaotic hallucinations and therefore not fully responsible. Responsibility, it was said, lay rather with the German people, which lacked 'instinct', was naturally inclined to force and extremism, had been brought up in a tradition of blind obedience and therefore sold itself to a politician whose chaotic ideas led to a *Götterdämmerung* on earth. It had given proof of these tendencies in two world wars.

The first theory shifts responsibility on to a metaphysical state of affairs; the object is to forget the whole thing. The second theory harps on the past, placing an entire people in the dock and making it an object of lasting suspicion. Neither theory, however, holds water; neither is objective or scientific. They do disservice both to the German people and to the brotherhood of man throughout the world.

Objective analysis of the vital years from 1930 to 1933 shows clearly that Hitler was no phenomenon endowed with supernatural powers; it also shows that, despite his demagogy and the conditions of the time, the German people gave proof of a considerable degree of political instinct and political maturity, at least as long as it was living under normal conditions and could choose its political leaders freely.

From both Breiting's interviews it is clear that Hitler had worked out his plans beforehand with sliderule precision. He counted upon a coalition with the 'national opposition', in other words with the German Nationalist Peoples Party, and thanks to this coalition he succeeded in seizing power. Exactly as he had forecast in talking to Breiting, he was supported in his claim to power by industry and some senior officers. By thumping the anti-communist drum, by the end of 1932 he was able to face the bourgeoisie with the ostensible alternative 'Bolshevism or National-Socialism'. Anyone bold enough to dismiss this as unrealistic on the grounds that communists only formed one-eighth of the electorate, was branded as a traitor to the nation. The cry 'Bolshevism or National-Socialism' was directed primarily against the Centre Party and the Social Democrats. Its object was to cripple these and other democratic parties and so undermine the Weimar Republic.

Brüning, who had been Chancellor since 1930, was ruling without Social Democrat support and therefore by emergency legislation, a practice by no means unwelcome to Hitler both for political and juridical reasons. In fact it smoothed the way for him ultimately to break up the 'black-red' coalition existing in the Prussian Chamber of Deputies. It provided him with a basis for his 'legal' seizure of power – without agreement from people or parliament.[1]

From 1923 to 1929 that great statesman Stresemann had pursued a policy which had gained his country authority and respect both at home and abroad. But this method of conducting government business was rejected, not only by Hitler, but also by many in conservative circles. In October 1925 Stresemann signed the Treaty of Locarno (Germany – France – Great Britain – Belgium – Italy) fixing frontiers in the west and laying down security guarantees. In April 1926 he signed a Pact of Friendship with Russia.[2] In September 1926 his efforts culminated in the reconciliation with France, Briand declaring that 'rifles and guns' had been replaced by 'peace and conciliation'. Stresemann was the first to hail Briand's pan-Europe policy, strove for economic collaboration between France and Germany, and was a protagonist of general disarmament. In August 1928 he signed the Kellogg Pact outlawing war; only premature death prevented him pursuing the policy he had initiated.

In spite of Stresemann's success the conservatives had

never approved his 'Fulfilment' policy. A few months before
his death he had accepted the Young Plan limiting reparations payments and setting a term to them – though admittedly
a long one – and had thereby achieved the evacuation of the
Rhineland; this, however, led to the formation of a real anti-
Stresemann front. Hugenberg and Hitler formed a 'National
Unity Front' to protest against the Young Plan and the
'enslavement of the German people' through reparations; they
tried to impeach Stresemann as signatory of the agreement.
At the ensuing plebiscite the attempt failed miserably, gaining
only 5·8 million votes, though admittedly the poll was very
small. Nevertheless Hitler had found his first platform for
the expansion of his power.

In September 1930, after years of the most violent agitation, Hitler could only score $6\frac{1}{2}$ million votes and he was
realist enough to recognise that the time for his seizure of
power was not yet. He realised that he would never succeed
in collecting the 'nationalist' votes for the NSDAP and that,
if he was to reach his goal, he must win over the conservative
upper middle class as temporary allies.[3]

For this purpose it was necessary to gain the goodwill of
the bourgeois press and the conversations with Richard
Breiting formed part of the effort to do so. They were part
of a tactical plan, stubbornly pursued.

When Hitler launched his assault on the bourgeois press,
his argument ran: With its $6\frac{1}{2}$ million voters the NSDAP is the
second strongest party. Unless they are shown some alternative, the economic crisis will drive people in ever increasing
numbers into the arms of the communists. This alternative
is the NSDAP which will create 'sound conditions'.

Those whose job it was to infiltrate Hitler's ideas into the
major newspapers were good at their tactics. They maintained
that they must keep in touch with the Führer of the NSDAP
in order to detach the healthy forces within his movement
from the extremists and their economic plans. On 10 October
1931 the Munich correspondent of the *Deutsche Allgemeine*

Zeitung wrote that the entire NSDAP was still capable of development, that its economic programme was not yet firm and that 'the deadly enemy of communism had arisen' – despite the negative attitude of the bourgeoisie. Moreover, he continued, a man like Hitler must be 'brought into the team because of his energy and his enthusiasm for an improvement of conditions'.

The atmosphere after the 1930 elections, when Hitler captured 107 seats in the Reichstag, is illustrated by a letter to a friend from Bernhard, the Chairman of the Darmstädter and National Bank. Bernhard expressed the view that the National-Socialists 'could contribute to the removal of internal difficulties', though there was still some 'economic dirt' to be eliminated in the NSDAP. (Letter to Fritz Klein, 17 November 1930.) Bernhard thought it 'crazy' to attribute too much weight to Hitler's anti-semitism since 'the Jews themselves were to blame for anti-semitism'. The only people who might feel themselves affected by this anti-semitism were the aspirants to the 'world stage' – Carl von Ossietzky, for instance. Bernhard's alternatives at that time were 'worthwhile elements of the NSDAP' or 'a loathsome rule by party bosses' – meaning primarily the Social Democrats. On 1 December 1930 the *Deutsche Allgemeine Zeitung* felt able to publish a leading article headed 'Abdication of a System' – the parliamentary system. This influential newspaper published long extracts from *Mein Kampf*, calling the book 'an informative contribution'. In addition it published views from General von Seeckt and Hjalmar Schacht, the banker, both welcoming a government with Hitler in it.

As Richard Breiting sat opposite Hitler he knew that Brandi, a member of the German Peoples Party, had been violently critical of the international policy pursued by Curtius, the Foreign Minister, regarding him as an adherent of the 'fulfilment policy', in other words fulfilment of all obligations undertaken by Germany towards foreign countries. Hitler, on the other hand, was demanding immediate cessation of all reparations payments. Breiting also knew that Dingeldey, his party leader, saw nothing wrong in governing without the Reichstag under certain circumstances and that von Papen's circle was urging a change in the constitution. Pressure on Hindenburg from the 'national opposition' was increasing all the time with ever louder cries for the dismissal of Curtius, Treviranus, Wirth, Schiele and Dietrich. In support of this campaign Hitler and Göring were continually lobbying in the wings. Göring, as an Air Force captain, importuned Hindenburg to stop the agitation against his party, pointing out that it had the support of $6\frac{1}{2}$ million voters and should be given its due place in the state. Hugenberg, the leader of the German Nationals, maintained that 'even a dictator government must have some backing from the people'. Thus it came about that Kirdorf, the great industrialist, invited Hitler and forty representatives of major firms to his estate in the country. On 10 September 1931, three months after Breiting's interview, Hitler met Brandi, Vögler, Thyssen and others for a discussion in the Berlin 'Kaiserhof'. The instigator of this meeting was Otto Dietrich, the same man who had arranged the Hitler-Breiting interviews. Exactly a month later the dignitaries of the 'national opposition' (German Nationals, Stahlhelm and Brandi of the Peoples Party) met Hitler in Harzburg. The 'Harzburg Front' was formed, and Hitler had reached a vital stage on his road to power.

Breiting was not, of course, the only man to whom Hitler revealed his thoughts; he did so to other selected representatives of the German bourgeoisie. We do not, however, possess notes of these other interviews. Breiting's shorthand therefore fills a gap in our knowledge of Hitler's tactics when dealing with the conservatives. Basically he despised them but wished to use them as a draught horse. Whether speaking to an officer, an industrialist or a press representative, he undoubtedly used the same arguments, but the conversation, consisting primarily of monologues, would be geared to the profession of whomever he was interviewing.

Hitler's statements to Breiting show clearly how far he had revealed his plans and intentions to his future partners in the coalition. They did not act in ignorance of what was coming to them. They were fully informed and at first hand.

The German people's great tragedy lay in the fact that Hitler's ideas awoke echoes in many circles. The conservatives, for instance, were unwilling to admit either war guilt or that the First World War defeat had been a military one; many of the millions returning from the front regarded Versailles, the occupation of the Rhineland and the Ruhr, and the limitation of the German armed forces as a national disgrace. Right wing circles had never accepted the Weimar constitution and pressed openly for a change both in the constitution and in voting rights. They could not bring themselves to support Stresemann's conciliatory policy or to share responsibility for internal affairs with the Centre, still less with the Social Democrats. They thought it beneath their national dignity to work with the socialists for a solution of the state problem.

Hitler was, of course, wily enough to draw a sharp distinction between his 'confidential' revelations to selected people and his exposés of his programme to the German people or the outside world. This was the reason for the promise extracted from Breiting not to publish the talks as a press interview. The reference to the resulting loss of advertisement custom which Hitler pretended the newspaper might suffer, was a mere pretext. Nothing could have been more unwelcome to Hitler than some publication unmasking the plans and intentions concealed behind his clichés of 'peace and honour' or 'work and daily bread'.

If Hitler was to appeal to the broad mass of the people he was bound to present himself as a socialist and promise 'socialistic measures'.[4] Only the initiated such as Breiting knew how indifferent he was to these points in his programme. Hitler regarded elections and swaying the masses merely as a sort of repeated turning of the soil. 'A statesman must cultivate his people year by year as a farmer does his fields' (16 October 1932). Nevertheless, as his talk with Breiting shows, he was under no illusion that the workers would vote in his favour – at least as long as the Social Democrat and communist parties were still in existence. He repeatedly said, of course, that the Third Reich[5] must be established, not by princes, but by the people. By the word 'people', however, he meant himself or what he intended to turn the people into.

Convinced that he was a historical genius destined to remodel both the people and the world, Hitler believed that he was one of those 'world-history individuals' who need take no account of moral or juridical considerations.[6] The great conquerors such as Hannibal, Alexander the Great, Caesar, Ghengis Khan or Napoleon had never for a moment thought of giving account of their decisions to anyone. Decisions of world-historical scope, however, could only be taken once Hitler finally had the power in his own hands.

His view of the foreign situation was as wide of the mark as his judgement of the internal political conditions for the development of his power was accurate. On this point he failed even to convince Breiting. As editor of a major German newspaper Breiting knew the foreign situation better than Hitler and made no secret of his views, but Hitler waved them away as pessimism. This did not reduce Breiting's respect for Hitler's rhetorical ability, however; Hitler undoubtedly possessed extraordinary oratorical and organisational talent.[7] He was the brain and the driving force of the NSDAP and from the outset regarded himself as the Leader of an all-embracing germanic 'movement' standing above party.

At the time when Hitler explained his plans to Breiting the bourgeois right-wing parties already regarded the Führer of this 'movement' as the man with whom they would have to work one day. They agreed with his diagnosis that the Weimar Republic was worn out and on its deathbed. The communist threat was not the primary reason for the formation of the 'Harzburg Front' in October 1931; it was the thought of the legacy which the dying republic was likely to leave behind it. Though the majority knew that Hitler's all-or-nothing policy ('I demand total subjection') constituted a danger, they hoped that he was pitching his demands high in order to win votes and that his extravagant plans would be cut down to size when face to face with reality. If, they thought, his seizure of power was to take place by 'legal means' – and there was no question of anything else – then Hitler would have to take some account of the wishes of his partners in government.

Hitler knew perfectly well that, if he continually referred to 'legal means', he could reassure anyone he was talking to. To Breiting he went so far as to mention a reconciliation with the bourgeoisie. This forthcoming attitude was based upon a highly realistic appreciation of his strength in early summer 1931.

Hitler was not yet a German citizen and the Bavarian government had no intention of assisting him to become one. On the other hand he knew that it would be difficult for them to act against a stateless person who nevertheless had volunteered for service in the First World War and had won the Iron Cross Second Class in 1914 and First Class in 1918. He could boast nearly $6\frac{1}{2}$ million voters. Yet he was looked on an an upstart with a woolly programme.

The bourgeois press adopted a wait-and-see attitude. Hindenburg and the Reichswehr were by no means ready to opt for Hitler. More important still, however, his organisation had not yet reached the stage when a final assault would be likely to succeed. On 1 January 1931 the SA and SS numbered only 100,000 and on the day of the September elections Hitler's party membership was only 293,000. Yet on 1 January 1932, six months after his interview with Breiting, the SA and SS had reached 300,000 and the Party had 800,000 members.[8] What had happened? Where had this brown-shirted flood come from?

In the forefront stood the economic crisis which had spilled over from America into Germany. This made the reparations burden appear even more oppressive, an argument which Hitler knew how to turn to his own advantage. When the government proposed to approve a credit for the construction of Battle-cruiser A, the Social Democrat parliamentary party criticised its whole defence policy. But neither officials, petty bourgeoisie nor the unemployed regarded this as any contribution to the solution of the crisis. Even the Socialists' demand for an increase in unemployment insurance contributions seemed to offer no way out of the difficulties. When the Socialists then went into opposition in 1930 in order to capture the votes of the discontented, this did not improve their prospects. The Brüning government, being a minority régime, ruled by authoritarian methods; it was looked on as a makeshift which could not and should not last long. With his emergency legislation based on the 'exceptional situation' clause in the constitution and his austerity measures such as the reduction of official salaries, Brüning failed to produce a change. He became known as the 'Starvation Chancellor' and unemployment rose. The petty bourgeoisie, the officials and the unemployed drew their conclusions.

By 1932 the number of NSDAP members had almost reached the figure set by Hitler as necessary for the forthcoming street battles; he had not, however, either the organisation or the intelligence service indispensable for the seizure of power. He needed to influence the press and make his own Party news-sheets viable. In addition he wished to gain a footing in the Reichswehr, industry, the universities and the police. For all this Hitler required time and money, as he admitted to Breiting. He also had to proceed with caution *vis-à-vis* the outside world. The British in particular must not become suspicious. Italian approval of his policy was more or less assured – and in *Mein Kampf* he had said: 'For a long time yet to come there will be only two powers in Europe with which it may be possible for Germany to conclude an alliance. These powers are Great Britain and Italy.'

French policy Hitler considered, was inspired by hatred and dictated by Jews; he therefore expected no support from that quarter. He believed, however, that he could afford to disregard the opinion of France.

During 1932 the National-Socialist leader continued to build up his SA, his SS and his intelligence service under Reinhard Heydrich; he perfected the 'fifth column' methods later used both at home and abroad. It was not long before Himmler and Heydrich were able to give him considerable insight into the police, the Reichswehr, industry, the press and the Reich President's circle. Hitler came to the conclusion that the bourgeoisie was composed of various groups, each of which was jealously defending its position and interests. He therefore infiltrated into various levels of society with the object of promising all of them guarantees and opportunities for their future development. NSDAP headquarters, so he assured his future coalition partners, would not be promoted to the status of a super-Party agency. The 'national concentration' should throw up strong personalities and they, armed with the authority of the State and their position in the government, would be 'true masters' of their departments and finally put some order into the State. This implied that the Ministers of the Reich would not be dependent on political party gnomes. This government should last at least a year and should exercise power unhampered by party or Reichstag ballots. On 28 January 1933 Hitler did, of course, assure von Papen that everything would be done legally and constitutionally. In saying this, however, he had not the smallest intention of leaving Ministries in the hands of his partners for any length of time; they were doomed to dismissal and he did not propose to give them time to re-establish their authority in the country. For him they were simply the Trojan horse from which he would himself emerge. The

104

gift which he proffered to the bourgeois party leaders was in fact a powder barrel. Hitler could well afford his promise to seize power legally and take account of the popular will, for he knew beforehand that he would have captured the most important departments of state, the Ministry of the Interior and the Prussian police; he also knew that his organisation would have achieved the necessary strength and offensive capability and that he could then move a step nearer total power by means of a well-staged act of provocation to serve as pretext for his *coup d'état*.[9]

Even today certain intellectuals still propound the idea that Hitler had no need of the Reichstag fire since he was already in power. Had he really wished to carry out a *coup d'état*, they say, he would have engineered it before the seizure of power. But this view is wrong; until he was Chancellor and had the power, Hitler would not and could not strike against Hindenburg, the Reichswehr, the State and the masses who were still under the influence of their party leaders.

Instead Hitler wished to demonstrate that he was a worthy partner for the powers that be. Of these the most important was the Reichswehr, regarded as a factor for law and order because of the part it had played in tiding over the crisis. Its influence had grown considerably since the election of Hindenburg to the Presidency in 1925. Right-wing organisations such as the Stahlhelm worked closely with the Reichswehr. As early as 16 December 1926 Philipp Scheidemann of the Socialist Party had attacked reactionary Reichswehr elements for intriguing against Stresemann's efforts and policy. A public protest took place on the occasion of the dedication of the Tannenberg Memorial on 18 September 1928, when the Social Democrat organisation 'Reichsbanner' refused to take part because Ludendorff was to appear. Hindenburg made a nationalistic speech. As the years went by voices were raised saying that the Reichswehr was a state within the state. Hitler took good account of all this and therefore had nothing but words of praise for the Reichswehr as a whole. He was not, of course, unaware of the rivalries between the Generals. On the pretext of protecting the Reichswehr from political interference he protested loudly against the defence credits as being too small. He stated repeatedly that his para-military formations would be available for the defence of the country. Numerous officers worked with Hitler's defence experts and prepared studies proving that neither internal peace nor external defence could be assured unless the volunteer formations were included in the mobilisation plan. So-called pre-military training was introduced and Röhm was assiduous in establishing contact with the Generals. From Hitler's point of view the object of these manoeuvres was to let some of his men 'feed off the Reichswehr field kitchens', infiltrate his people into the military intelligence network and win over the Reichswehr as an ally for his claim to power.

The importance which Hitler attributed to the Reichswehr was shown in 1932 when he demanded the dissolution of the Reichstag. On 4 June 1932 he entered into consultation with General Schleicher, the Reichswehr Minister, and it was to him that the memorandum was delivered stressing that the composition of the Reichstag no longer represented the will of the people and the existing position could profit only the communists. The very next day, on 5 June, Hindenburg signed the dissolution order. Hitler had known whom to turn to at the right moment in order to get his way. Schleicher received no recompense for his assistance.

At about this time certain Reichswehr officers were campaigning for rearmament and the 'black army'. One of the protagonists was Lieutenant-Colonel Ott, a confidant of Schleicher's, whom Hitler did reward for his pains after 1933. Being an intelligence expert he rose to be ambassador in Japan; unfortunately he became so embroiled in secret service work that he confided in a Soviet agent named Sorge and gave away all manner of secrets.[10]

Neither the fall of the Brüning government nor the for-

mation of von Papen's cabinet suited Hitler at all. His grapevine propagandists spread the rumour that Ministers had
only been appointed with Hitler's agreement and that they
would only remain in office pending the dissolution of the
Reichstag and the calling of fresh elections. Thereafter a
new government would be formed based on an absolute
majority of the NSDAP and German Nationals. As it turned
out Hitler was right: the Reichstag was in fact dissolved,
new elections were called for 31 July 1932 and the main
slogan of the electoral campaign was 'National unity versus
ruin'.

In his manifesto Hitler accused the Centre Party and the
Social Democrats of patent 'cheating' because they had
changed the Prussian Landtag's rules for the election of the
Minister-President. On 24 April 1932 the Centre and
Socialists had decided that the nomination of Minister-President should be by overall majority, whereas previously he
had been elected by simple majority. The new situation meant
that the old rules gave no advantage to the strongest party.
The National-Socialists then accused the black-red front of
'persecuting and oppressing' the NSDAP with the object of
perpetuating the 'rake's economy', already prevalent for
fourteen years, until bankruptcy was reached. Nevertheless,
they said, Providence would ensure that Hitler and his friends
had an absolute majority and that a new government would
come into existence on 1 August 1932.

In order to prepare the electorate for the great day Hitler
decided to give people an impressive show. In addition to
attempts by the SS and SA to provoke clashes, Goebbels and
Göring hit upon the idea of organising a 'freedom flight over
Germany' by the Führer. In his aircraft No. D 1720 Hitler
flew from city to city showing that he was a man who kept
abreast of technical progress. Over some cities he organised
real stunt flights accompanied by certain industrialists in
their private aeroplanes; he inspected the latest machines
and visited the giant flying boat 'Do X' in Warnemünde, a

photograph of him doing so appearing in every newspaper.

For the crowd awaiting him in the Weser Stadium in Bremen he had a special scenario – his brilliantly lighted aircraft swept several times across the night sky. This shining apparition in the heavens was obviously meant to indicate that God had endowed the Germans with technical capacity of the highest order and, in addition to the products of their unique ability, had also presented them with a Messiah. Hitler was forever repeating in his speeches that he was not interested in seats in parliament or ministerial offices but in German men and women, in their honour, peace, work and daily bread. The intellectuals he tried to win over by saying that 'preservation of the intellect is the prerequisite for the struggle against the decay and ruin of the Reich'; and again 'The scientific achievements of German genius have been used in the interests of Jewish world finance'. Under his leadership all this would be brought to an end and unheard-of progress achieved. 'The prerequisite is the reorganisation of our racial community and the preservation of our race.'[11] Hitler promised to place machines at the service of peace and the production of daily bread. As soon as German technicians and workers had constructed a mighty production machine, however, Göring screamed: 'Guns first, then butter.'

A Hitler fighting for work and daily bread was just what the voters were looking for. His 'freedom flights' marked him out as a politician susceptible to things modern and technical. Goebbels' agitators went further and created Führer legends; according to one of these the aircraft's direction-finding gear had failed on one occasion but Hitler had been able by intuition to indicate the correct direction to the pilot and so had saved the aircraft and its complement from catastrophe.

Hitler claimed that he was unable to address the people direct because use of the radio had been denied him; he therefore recorded his call to the nation on gramophone records (the first he ever made) and hundreds of thousands of these were distributed by his agitators to towns and villages which he was not scheduled to visit himself. The 'call' was also broadcast by loud-speaker. People were thereby given the impression that it was in fact unfair that the NSDAP was not allowed to use the radio. Hitler's gramophone record announced that he was fighting against the division of the nation and had only one aim: to form a popular community despite the attempt of international finance to divide the German people. He proposed to bring nationalism and socialism together. 'In those November days of 1918 they promised solemnly to lead our people, and in particular the German worker, into a better economic future. Having had nearly fourteen years to make good their promises, they cannot today call upon a single German profession to bear witness to any good that they have done. The German farmer is pauperised, the middle class ruined, the social aspirations of millions destroyed, one-third of the working population unemployed and so without means of livelihood.'

In his speech recorded in the studio and employing every trick of rhetoric, he implored the middle class, the farmers, the intellectuals, the Catholics and the Protestants to work for Germany's future without distinction of class, calling or beliefs. Sarcastically his voice rang from the gramophone: 'The middle class is supposed to be saved from ruin by the middle class parties and the economy by the economic parties. The Catholic is supposed to take refuge with the Centre and the Protestant with the Christian Socialist Peoples Party. Eventually landlords will have their own political representation like the tenants, the employees and the officials.' Then Hitler turned to pathos: 'If Germany goes down, there will be no social paradise in which the worker may flourish nor will it be found by the entrepreneur; the farmer will not be able to save himself nor will the middle class.' The record was a best-seller; it cost only 5 marks and brought the Führer's voice to the listener for $8\frac{1}{2}$ minutes.[12]

During this period clashes in the streets were of unparal-

leled violence. Hitler accused Otto Braun, the Regierungs-
präsident [government representative] in Prussia, of seeking
to influence the elections by persecuting and oppressing
National-Socialists. It was almost equivalent to a *coup
d'état*, he said. Following an agreement between the von
Papen government and the Reichswehr Hindenburg signed
an ordinance, based on Article 48 of the Constitution, 'For
the Re-establishment of public Law and Order'. The von
Papen government thereupon commissioned Lieutenant-
General von Rundstedt, commanding Reichswehr Group
Headquarters I in Berlin, to relieve the Prussian ministers
and officials of their appointments and arrest them in their
offices.[13]

These measures were taken on 20 July 1932, eleven days
before the elections. Their effect on certain categories of voter
was favourable to Hitler, since many of the less ideologically
influenced farmers, middle class and officials, hitherto standing aloof, saw in them the long-awaited 'end to anarchy'. The
fact that the disturbances had been provoked by the SA and
SS was immaterial to much of the electorate. If Hindenburg
and the Reichswehr wished to re-establish order, they
thought, one could not but approve the steps they took.
Hitler, in any case, expected much from these measures and
calculated on a vast increase in votes. For a few days Hindenburg and von Papen had declared a state of emergency and
had had some tiresome politicians arrested. NSDAP headquarters forecast a total of 17-20 million votes.

Hitler's disappointment was therefore great when on 31
July 1932 he was forced to admit that, despite all his efforts
and the favourable factors, he had gained a mere 300,000
votes. At the second ballot in the Presidential elections of
April 1932 he had already scored 13·4 million. Nevertheless
the NSDAP was now the strongest party with 36·7 per cent of
the electorate. Hitler and his advisers immediately set about
analysing the other parties' electoral results and they came
to the following conclusions:

EPILOGUE

1. The propaganda employed had been inadequate to detach the mass of the people from their traditional parties – the Centre, the Bavarian Peoples Party, the Socialist Party and the Communist Party.

2. The 'bolshevism or National-Socialism' alternative had not been put over forcefully enough in the streets to drive to the polls a sufficient proportion of that section of the electorate which was indifferent, passive, but nevertheless averse to communism.

3. The people as a whole could only be converted if political power went hand in hand with control of the press and radio.

It was also clear to Hitler and his associates that, if they were to be more successful at the next elections, in addition to control of the radio and press they must have martyrs.

Between 14 September 1930 and 31 July 1932 Hitler had raised his party's vote from 6·4 million to 13·7 million, the highest figure he ever achieved under democratic rules. What had happened to double the number of his supporters in two years? Was it the result of the fiendish force of his personality or of the German people's 'lack of instinct'? Thirty per cent of the electorate, 13 million men, had testified to their confidence in Hitler. Did they know and approve his programme? What was the composition of this section of the population?

It would be both unjust and inaccurate to accuse this mass of people of having approved Hitler's authoritarian methods, his bellicose policy or his anti-semitism. It would also be wrong to say that they were a mere collection of opportunists and thugs. Of the 13·7 million there were probably no more than 500,000 whose main aim in life was to wear a uniform and take part in propaganda marches on pretext of contributing to the defence of their country which was not allowed enough soldiers. Extremists of this type are to be found in all countries. The majority of Hitler's party members consisted of discontented and misguided idealists.

Hitler's movement and his following were the reverse of a homogeneous political group. He himself called the Weimar Republic parties a 'rats-tail' but the term could well have been applied to his own jumble of adherents which included all malcontents from the National Revolutionaries on the extreme left to the monarchists on the extreme right. Otto Strasser's supporters campaigned for socialist reform of the economy, the ex-Free Corps officers dreamed of the reconstitution of a powerful army and disputed Hitler's claim to future leadership; the SS loyalists proclaimed a mythology of the blood at the head of which Hitler, the divine being, would take the place of Wotan.

The Junkers, heavily in debt, saw a chance of offloading their mortgages. The Generals counted upon the reintroduction of military service and an increase of military credits. The monarchists – Herbert-Otto von Bismarck, for instance – staked their cards on the recall of the Hohenzollerns. So there was nothing so extraordinary in the facts that the Hohenzollern Prince August-Wilhelm was to be seen marching in SA formations, that in April 1932 at Oels the ex-Crown Prince called upon the monarchists to vote for Adolf Hitler at the second ballot of the Reich Presidential elections, or that in 1933 Hermine, the Kaiser's second wife, hastened from Holland to Berlin to greet the new Chancellor with 'Heil Hitler'. In April 1932 this entire 'rats-tail' was able to capture 13·4 million votes out of a total of 37·6 million. The 6·5 million who did not vote were not at this time Hitler supporters.

In the summer of 1932 Hitler's demagogic promises had a number of factors in their favour:

1. His forecasts of unemployment had proved correct. Five to six million men were on national assistance. The unemployed reckoned upon Hitler providing them with means of livelihood again, not only in industry, but also in the SA, the Wehrmacht and the police which Hitler had promised to take over. The petty bourgeoisie, hard hit by the crisis

and living a precarious existence, saw Hitler as their saviour; he had promised to smash the trusts and monopolies and eliminate the competition from the Jewish chain stores. His 'new order', it was thought, would raise living standards.

2. Industry regarded Hitler as the man to consult in settling the social problems. On 27 January 1932 he presented his programme to industry, announcing himself as the saviour, and shortly thereafter the Party coffers began to fill. The industrialists counted upon an economic revival as a result of his rearmament plans.

3. The Right agreed with Hitler about the 'failure' of social democracy. Its 'party bosses', they said, overruled the 'decent officials' and with its wages and unemployment insurance policies it was creating a 'bottomless pit'.

4. The nationalist formations wanted a national coalition. Hitler took his stand on the spirit of the Harzburg Front. Many officers and NCOs no longer required by the Weimar Republic's little army but still clinging to the military tradition, had found employment as commanders of SA and SS units.

5. Bavaria having refused to naturalise Hitler, Brunswick had made him a German citizen on 25 February 1932. This enabled Hitler to stand as candidate for the Reich Presidency in two ballots. In the light of Hindenburg's advanced age many sections of the population thought that between a marxist or National-Socialist candidate Hitler was the lesser of two evils.

6. Hitler's campaign against Groener, the Reichswehr Minister, and Brüning, the Chancellor, had borne fruit. Both these politicians lost their offices. Von Papen was ruling as Chancellor without a Reichstag majority and campaigning for a change in the constitution which would have split the parties by bringing in a new electoral law. The rapid changes of government, none of which were in control of the situation, led to the desire for some authority. Mussolini was an example.

7. With its social harmony and low unemployment rate Fascist Italy appeared a model which Germany might well copy. Moreover a corporative system would be in line with the interests of the Christian working population. Germany had had many authoritarian régimes as neighbours – in Poland, Bulgaria, Yugoslavia, Turkey, Greece and Portugal. Foreign countries also wished to see some 'consolidation' in Germany. Hitler was applauded by many fascist groups, particularly in Holland, Belgium, France and Hungary. These later provided the collaborators who handed the Jewish population over to Himmler's executioners. As a statesman Hitler had made the greatest impression on certain people in British society. In 1932 Churchill had already travelled to Munich to meet him – but in vain; Hitler would not receive him.

8. Hitler coupled his anti-communist propaganda with accusations against the Jews, as came crudely to light in his conversations with Breiting. The facts, for instance, that Willi Münzenberg edited a communist illustrated and that certain intellectuals regarded communism as a defence against Nazism enabled Hitler to say that the communist party was a militant organisation supported by international Jewish finance and aiming to hold Germany down in misery and shame for ever.

Hitler would have been only too pleased to see clashes between Social Democrats and communists, as also an assault by the communist party on the bourgeoisie. Disturbances with traffic paralysed, shops and houses looted and political personalities murdered would have been more than welcome to him; on the basis of Article 48 of the constitution he could then have incorporated his paramilitary formations into the official machine. One of the SA slogans was: 'Look, you unemployed, the communist party takes no action against the bourgeoisie because it is supported by Jewish finance. German communists dare not act because the Moscow bureaucrats tell them not to!' Hitler attempted to play up the role of the renegades, to mobilise the extreme left-wing organisations and use them for direct action. This would have enabled him to say to the electorate, which was longing for peace and quiet: 'Look where "democracy" is leading you.' Every crime was laid at the door of the communists and Jews. One or two Jews were attacked on the streets by Hitler's thugs. Only after the Reichstag fire and his seizure of power, however, could he 'organise' the Jewish boycott of 1 April 1933 and not until he had been dictator for five and a half years could he set light to the synagogues, and even then it was done by Reinhard Heydrich's special detachments.

The most effective theme of Hitler's propaganda from 1930 to 1932, however, was his campaign against the *diktat* of Versailles and even more the burden of war debts and reparations. By his fighting speeches against the reparations burden he turned himself into the advocate of salvation and restoration of the German economy. Admittedly the 132 milliard mark total required from Germany under the 1921 London Agreement had been replaced by the Dawes Plan of 1924 which mentioned no fixed sum; admittedly annual assessments were now the cry and the Young Plan of 1930 had reduced the total figure to 60 milliard. Nevertheless continuous invective about reparations charges formed a good platform for Hitler in his attempt to influence those sections of the population on which the burden of payment fell. To keep the record straight it must be admitted that between 1924 and the summer of 1931 Germany had in fact paid France almost 6 milliard, England 2·3 milliard, Italy 800 million, Belgium 750 million and other countries about 1·4 milliard – 11·2 milliard in all. Hitler calculated that between 1930 and 1988 Germany would have to pay a further 114·5 milliard direct, in interest on loans or in compound interest. According to his calculations this came to 2 milliard per year – as he told Breiting.

When addressing the unemployed Hitler's speakers reduced

the problem to the simplest terms, explaining that if Germany did not have to pay this levy, they could each receive 500 marks a year more. No word about these promises to the unemployed was said to the farmers; they were promised interest-free credits to deal with the agricultural crisis. To the industrialists the hope was held out that they might invest this sum in their businesses. This campaign was so successful that even the Social Democrats and communists began to agitate for the abolition of war debts. To illustrate the enormity of the burden Hitler's agitators talked of enslavement of the second and third generations – 'You, your children and your grandchildren will still have to pay.' When the moratorium proposed by Hoover came into force (11 July 1931 to 30 June 1932) Hitler's propagandists were jubilant as if this victory had been due to them. The Lausanne Reparations Agreement (9 July 1932) fixed the war debt at 3 milliard marks. Germany, however, was still liable for servicing the loan and for interest at a cost of several hundred million. Hitler could therefore still use an attack on this expenditure as the basis for his speeches. He did not, of course, for a moment consider using these '2 milliard' saved by the abolition of reparations for the benefit of the unemployed or the workers. He was quite frank with Breiting, who after all had come to him as a representative of the bourgeoisie: 'As you will realise, I cannot say that at a public meeting.' He assured Breiting that these 2 milliard were nothing like so important as the 18 milliard additional expenditure forced on the government by the trade unions over the three years 1925 to 1928. The two payments together meant that the state was squandering 8 milliard annually. This electoral carrot, dressed up to suit the views of the individual audience, was dangled before the various categories of voter at various meetings. One of Breiting's criticisms was that each one of Hitler's speakers presented his economic and social programme differently, to which Hitler replied that he could not prescribe what each individual should say and in any case all the bourgeoisie had to do was to put 10 million marks into his Party treasury and he would then ensure that his propaganda was consistent. This was no more than a disguised invitation to the bourgeoisie: 'Make me the mouthpiece of your class and then you will have no more to fear from my speakers' demagogue methods.' His protestations that he could save the nation from catastrophe were aimed at the unemployed, the middle class, the officials and the war wounded. To the Christians he held up the bogey of communism. The elections of 31 July 1932 demonstrated who in the general confusion had been misled by Hitler's demagogy:

	Votes
The German National Peoples Party lost	300,000
The Christian National Peasants Party	1,000,000
The Landbund	100,000
The Christian-Social Peoples Service (an evangelical movement)	500,000
The Christian-Social Reich Party	230,000
The German Peoples Party	1,100,000
German Middle Class Party (Economic Party)	1,200,000
German State Party (a democratic party)	1,000,000
German Peasants Party	200,000
German-Hanoverian Party	100,000

The major Christian parties such as the Centre and the Bavarian Peoples Party on the other hand increased their vote, the former by 10 per cent, the latter by 20 per cent. The Social Democrats and Communists maintained their overall figure. Sections of the population, therefore, which had been hard hit by the crisis but had no definite ideological views, refused to vote for Hitler.

How unstable Hitler's support was is proved by the fact that three months later, at the 6 November 1932 elections, two million voters returned to their old parties – and this happened after von Papen had offered Hitler the Vice-Chancellorship and Hindenburg had received him as the leader of the strongest political party.

With his 13·7 million votes Hitler had achieved a solid base from which to risk a further advance. On 13 August 1932 von Papen summoned him to Berlin for a conference and he then had an audience of Hindenburg. Hitler took care to announce that he proposed to carry on his fight by fair means. When, however, von Papen offered him the Vice-Chancellorship and proposed various departments for other National-Socialist politicians, Hitler refused the offer. He demanded positions proportionate to the strength of his party, in other words he wished to take over the government.

Seizure of power by legal means having failed, Hitler felt it incumbent upon him to offer some excuse to all those who had voted for him. He accordingly gave an interview to the influential conservative industrial newspaper, the *Rheinisch-Westfälische Zeitung* of Essen which had supported his participation in the government; he accused the existing government of evading any reconstruction because, as Papen had told him, 'the Reich President had rejected his conditions beforehand'. He stated in the interview that he had not wished to put his arguments forward to the President. But this is not true.[14] In fact Hitler wished to show the country once and for all that he had now become a political personality over whom even the great Field Marshal Hindenburg could not ride roughshod. The fact that the Reich President had already decided to fob him off with a sinecure, the Vice-Chancellorship, was of no interest to him.

In Hitler's eyes the decisive fact was that the ex-corporal had been thought worthy of an audience of the Reich President. Going further still, he wished to foster the impression that in future the Reich would be ruled by a two-man team, Field Marshal – Corporal, Reich President – Reich Chancellor; an election poster produced after the Reichstag fire characterised this meeting as historic. The mass of the people, after all, was not yet conditioned to the 'One People, One Reich, One Führer' principle.

For this reason, in his interview with the *Rheinisch-West-fälische Zeitung*, Hitler's main criticism was that the government should think that the strongest party would be content with the Vice-Chancellorship. He did not, of course, mention the fact that his nomination as Chancellor would have ridden roughshod over the wishes of the majority of the people – the 63 per cent who had voted for the other parties – to say nothing of his secret determination to misuse the Chancellorship to destroy the parliamentary system. He tried to convince people of the righteousness of his claim as follows: 'In any case it was previously the rule in Germany that the leader of the largest party was charged with the formation of a cabinet; recently, however, the criterion for statesman-like qualities seems to have become, not the strength, but the weakness of a party.' With a play on Bismarck's words he added: 'Politics is no longer the art of the possible but has become the art of the impossible.'

He referred to 'ghastly political apparitions' and quite openly refused to content himself with the bird in the hand when there were obviously two in the bush. 'I shall never sell my birthright for a mess of pottage. My commanders would never understand me, had I acted otherwise.'[15]

Hitler regarded the elections called for 6 November 1932 by the von Papen cabinet as an opportunity to test the people's reaction to the government's 'undemocratic' proceedings. He accordingly spread the word: The offer of the Vice-Chancellorship and the conditions attached to it are merely a means of preventing the 'national concentration'.

In preparation for the forthcoming elections Hitler did all he could to rouse the masses. The fact that he had been received by Hindenburg he regarded as an important step towards the Chancellorship. His thugs appeared on streets once more searching for opportunities of provoking violent clashes. At all costs Hitler wanted to increase his list of martyrs so that he could say that a group of conspirators tolerated by the State was using his movement as a scapegoat.

The November elections, however, were a defeat for the NSDAP. It lost 2 million votes and 34 seats in the Reichstag. The German Nationals won 15 seats and the communists 11. Conservative circles could not but observe that Hitler had failed to decimate the communists and that, on the contrary, his brutal methods had increased communist support. The Communist Party had captured almost 17 per cent of the electorate and 100 seats in the Reichstag. The bourgeois press began to have second thoughts and was far less inclined to hail Hitler as the saviour of the nation. The SA had even used their beat-up methods on the Stahlhelm, sensing in it a competitor.

The *Leipziger Neueste Nachrichten* had long been a supporter of Stresemann's foreign policy. It did not, however, wish openly to oppose the NSDAP. It regarded maintenance of the right-wing trend in Saxony as the over-riding consideration. It looked upon Hitler as the coming man and thought that further efforts should be made to 'make him a parliamentarian', as Edgar Herfurth had said to Breiting after the first interview. It was hardly surprising that the German Peoples Party and Dingeldey, its leader, should adopt such a position seeing that on 5 November 1931 Bishop Kaas, the leader of the Centre Party, had said: 'The primary aim of the party is the intellectual and political transformation of the National-Socialist Party into a real instrument of State policy.' Kaas was speaking for his own party, the Centre. One wonders whether he really felt an intellectual transformation to be possible after Hitler had published *Mein Kampf* and Rosenberg *Der Mythus des 20 Jahrhunderts.*

Of the 'national opposition' only one man realised before it was too late that Hitler intended to carry out a *coup d'état*;

this was Dr. Ernst Oberfohren, the German National parliamentary floor-leader. He was a friend of Breiting and the latter was able to convince him that Hitler proposed to do away with the parliamentary system in order to rule by force through his 'best brains'. Oberfohren was one of those people who do not change their views merely because they meet resistance. He therefore welcomed Hitler's refusal of the Vice-Chancellorship in von Papen's government. After it had become known that the NSDAP had lost 2 million votes in the November 1932 elections Oberfohren addressed the 'German Society' in Berlin on the internal political situation. He accused Hitler of having failed to win the proletariat over to the nation and of having driven the petty bourgeoisie to extremism through his demagogy. Oberfohren regarded the loss of 2 million votes as proof that the masses had turned away from Hitler once they realised that he was aiming at total power.

Oberfohren directed his attack on Goebbels as Hitler's evil genius, quoting his speech of 14 June 1932: 'Should a possibility of our rise to power present itself, an absolute prerequisite would be the closure of the Reichstag.' The German National politicians analysed Hitler's bids for power; they accused the NSDAP of threatening the republican system and called upon everyone to resist this party under all circumstances, even should it have 250 deputies in the Reichstag. By the time of Oberfohren's speech the number of National-Socialist deputies had sunk from 230 to 196 over a period of three months. He was therefore justified in regarding the future with optimism.

The problem which worried Oberfohren was the attitude of von Papen. His speech included the following: 'Ladies and gentlemen, I see one danger as far as the Papen government is concerned: I am not absolutely sure – this is of course confidential – whether under very severe pressure this government might not be liable to adopt other forms and methods; and the pressure might come from a party such as the National-Socialist which has really only increased in size as an anti-democratic movement. And yet it would have been so easy for this government to deal with the National-Socialist assault by re-establishing the primacy of political parties.' Oberfohren was even ready to challenge von Papen: 'It is now the duty of the government to act – and to act in the sense of Bismarck's words: "I regard as a despicable coward any Minister who is not prepared, if necessary, to stake both life and his honour to save his Fatherland even against the will of the majority." '[16]

Hitler was enraged by this speech; Goebbels thumped his propaganda drum even harder and the SA and SS provoked even more violent street battles. Secret messages were sent both to Hugenberg and to industry saying that the NSDAP would participate in a coalition only to save Germany from bolshevism. Hindenburg was old and had no wish to be forced to rule by emergency legislation. The National-Socialists upbraided him, saying that the only purpose served by a government which ruled by emergency decree and by-passed the Reichstag was to exclude the 'national opposition' from the affairs of state and encourage marxist intrigue. The NSDAP declared itself ready to participate in a national cabinet in which it had only two ministers, provided that Hitler was Reich Chancellor; it was prepared to leave to its coalition partners even important departments such as Economics, Finance, the Foreign Ministry, Justice and the Reichwehr; it was even ready to renounce in favour of von Papen the post of Reich Commissar for Prussia, important though it was. It demanded for itself only the Prussian police and the Ministry of the Interior and that only because it wished to be responsible for law and order during the revival of the economy and the reorganisation of the government machine.

To many supporters of the coalition this offer appeared to be proof of Hitler's moderation. Now, they thought, rearmament could at last begin under their control and the Reichs-

wehr be built up under a General such as Blomberg. Finally
an end would be put to interference with the economy by
the trade unions. In reality, of course, Hitler was determined
not to leave these departments in the hands of the 'Santa
Claus's' for long. He required a fake coalition cabinet to be
able to present himself to the people as the 'legal' Chancellor
– with Hindenburg's approval but without a parliamentary
majority. The increased authority this would give him would
enable him to use the Ministry of the Interior and the
Prussian police as he liked – and Prussia, which comprised
two-thirds of the Reich, had 200,000 men in its police.

Oberfohren saw through this game and realised at once
the threat to the Weimar Republic and the parliamentary
system. But the 'experts' who thought differently won the
day. Hindenburg eventually appointed the 'Bohemian Corporal' Chancellor with the agreement of Hugenberg, von
Papen and their backers in financial, industrial and military
circles. The spark had been lit on the fuse leading to World
War II and Auschwitz.

The office of Reich Chancellor, refused to Hitler when he
was at the height of his electoral success, was presented to
him at the very moment when the National-Socialist tide was
ebbing. The intermediary was Papen. What caused him to
exert his influence on Hindenburg? It is possible that he
thought Hitler's terms sensible. We would not wish to assume
that he knew what was in Hitler's mind as he departed with
his prize. Probably von Papen misappreciated the situation
and thought that Schleicher would be equally incapable of
succeeding where he had failed. Perhaps he merely wished
to change the constitution and the electoral law in order to
improve the conservatives' position. Nevertheless Oberfohren
had given Papen adequate warning that Hitler's primary
object in becoming head of government was to do away with
the parliamentary system. The fact that he nevertheless
agreed to become Vice-Chancellor in Hitler's government
shows that he had taken the risks into account and that in

his eyes destruction of the Weimar Republic outweighed the danger inherent in Hitler's claim to total power. He hoped to bury the sword of Damocles which hung over Germany by calling it a shining torch. It was a torch – but it was to set fire to the Reichstag.

In his recent book von Papen attempts to shift on to the shoulders of the German people the blame for the fact that he supported Hitler in his seizure of power. He says: 'Seeing that we have become used to looking at the events of that time through post-1945 spectacles, we find it distasteful to admit that a majority of the German people welcomed this government and its programme. Proof of this does not rest merely on the result of the 5 March 1933 elections.'[17] In saying this von Papen forgets that Hitler came to power with the support of a minority only;[18] he also forgets that between the decision to appoint Hitler (approved by von Papen) and the 5 March elections came the Reichstag fire, that between 27 February and 5 March 1933 tens of thousands of innocent people were carted off to prison or a concentration camp, that press and radio were under National-Socialist control and that the State machine had been purged of 'unhealthy elements' – and all because he, von Papen, in his capacity as Reich Commissar for Prussia, had authorised Göring to act. One would have hoped that von Papen would eventually have cleared up the background to the Reichstag fire, for he would have done the German people service thereby. In private correspondence with him I tried to get him to say what he knew but he refused to contribute to clarification of the greatest political crime of recent times. In one letter he did say that he could believe anything of the Nazis and that he would describe the events surrounding the Reichstag fire in his forthcoming book. To my astonishment I found that when the 400 pages of this book appeared, the fire was not even mentioned. In fact the book ends with the statement that the elections of 5 March 1933 must be regarded as an expression of the will of the people. The only explanation for his silence on this thorny problem must be that he wished to gloss over the fact that he had sat on the same government bench as the fire-raisers.[19]

Among the papers of von Papen's period as Chancellor has been found a speech which he made to a meeting of the *Volksdienst* in which he said: 'Yes, it is coming. The change in voting rights must come. I admit that it is thoroughly deplorable; my beloved Westphalian peasants would probably not elect Herr Hugenberg; provided that they had a von Papen list they would elect me straightaway – at least I think so. We do not propose to pretend, as many people say, that this Reichstag is a matter of no consequence to us; I do say, however, that we shall achieve our aim even if it cannot be done by parliamentary methods – and it will not be possible to do it that way. The country has a right to this assurance.'[20]

Breiting's papers show that Hugenberg's reasoning in favour of a coalition government with Hitler in it was as follows:

1. The government would be able to exert some influence on Hitler and thereby put a stop to the disturbances instigated by the SA and SS throughout Germany.

2. The German Nationals would have an overwhelming majority in the government and as Reich Commissar for Prussia, the largest *Land* comprising two-thirds of the Reich, Franz von Papen, a Catholic politician of the Centre, could bring direct influence to bear.

3. In his capacity as Minister of Economics Hugenberg proposed to control the entire economy.

4. Hugenberg declared himself ready, when a new government was formed, temporarily to ban the communist party in order to persuade Hitler to restrain the SA from terrorism on the streets. Hugenberg did in fact put these ideas forward at the cabinet meeting of 30 January 1933.

To the astonishment of his coalition partners, however,

Hitler demanded early new elections in which the communists would be permitted to participate. But this was merely cover for a disreputable electoral trick, the object of which only became clear after the elections. Hitler announced that he proposed to rule with the co-operation of the Reichstag and maintained that 'the political situation was highly favourable for the national coalition finally to obtain a 51 per cent parliamentary majority'. The majority of the cabinet were in no position to veto submission of the new policy to the people and it never occurred to them that they would thereby precipitate a crisis.

Oberfohren was well aware of Hitler's ideas from Breiting's talks and he accordingly warned Hugenberg of Hitler's plans. He was convinced that Hitler was planning some provocative act, some engineered coup, to take place before the 5 March elections to prevent them proceeding normally and ensure that they took place against the background of a supposed bolshevist assault. Oberfohren was in close touch with General Schleicher and his officers who ran a Germany-wide information system. In this intelligence service, unfortunately, were already people who had made a pact with Hitler, supported the new dictator and welcomed his rearmament plans enthusiastically. They were primarily the officers to whom Hitler had referred during his talks with Breiting. In the summer of 1931 Hitler could not yet know that Heydrich and Himmler would form so outstanding a team nor that they would establish contact with General Blomberg in Königsberg and his Chief of Staff Colonel von Reichenau. Now, however, Schleicher had ceased to be Reichswehr Minister and had been replaced by Blomberg who appointed von Reichenau head of his Ministerial Office. Schleicher would certainly never have placed transport at the disposal of the SA and SS to assist in their manhunt after political opponents on the night of the Reichstag fire.

Hitler had not the smallest intention of quarrelling with his cabinet colleagues about economic measures and so losing some of his authority. He was not out for a majority for the coalition but for himself, to enable him to form a government which would acknowledge him as absolute dictator. Only when he had become the unquestioned master could he mould the masses to his will. Despite all his propaganda he had not yet succeeded in rooting marxist ideology 'out of the workers' hearts and minds'. He had suffered a similar disappointment in the case of the Catholics and even with some of the liberal and conservative bourgeoisie.

He started with the electoral slogan: 'Creative capacity, not a majority, is decisive.' But he then decided to go into the elections with an even better plan and even more effective propaganda. He analysed the electorate and this taught him something.

He turned his attention to the floating vote, the politically undecided, to those who accept unquestioningly everything told them by the newspapers, the radio or the illustrated weekly. 'Numerically this group is by far the strongest, being composed of the broad masses of the people. Intellectually it forms the simplest portion of the nation. It cannot be classified according to occupation but only by grades of intelligence. Under this category come all those who have not been born to think for themselves or who have not learnt to do so and who, partly through incompetence and partly through ignorance, believe everything that is set before them in print.'[21] These were the 'lazybones', who from sheer 'mental idleness' were only too thankful to grasp at anything on which someone else had done the thinking. Hitler was determined not to be a Chancellor on the Müller, Brüning or von Papen model and he therefore decided to address himself to these 'lazybones' from a position of strength, with press and radio under his control. He thought the time had at last come to destroy the 'talking shop' and to present this provocative act as the first signal in a communist uprising. A more savage wave of arrests than von Papen's of 1932, monopoly of the press and radio which he had not got in July or November and the flames issuing from the Reichstag building would make a far greater impression on the 'lazybones' and blockheads than his lightning 'freedom flights' over Bremen, Königsberg, Kiel and other cities. Under these conditions the absolute majority, which had so far eluded him, must finally be achieved. The transformation of the regulation Chancellor into dictator would then only be a question of time.

Hitler's forecast proved correct. He succeeded in driving the 'lazybones' to the polls as never before. Hitler had to have an electoral victory in order to make good his promise to the entire world that he would come to power legally (his oath of 1930). He wished to play the honest broker, not only to the Germans but to the outside world, for his strategic objectives were not confined to the Reich frontiers. Hitler wished, indeed was forced, to influence the ideologically uncommitted section of the electorate and rouse the politically unstable elements. Such lazybones and turncoats are to be found over the length and breadth of the world.

Although at the 5 March elections held under the exceptional conditions following the Reichstag fire Hitler gained 5·5 million votes, he had still hardly won any from the Christian parties or the Social Democrats; his talk of imminent revolution had merely attracted some of the peasant and bourgeois voters. The real dupes were the 4 million who usually did not vote at all, the mass of the indifferent, the 'lazybones' who, as Hitler had said in *Mein Kampf*, believed anything printed and would always hunt with the hounds. These were the duped and the ignorant; to them were added people who, after Hitler's first show of power, were afraid to be registered as non-voters. From their point of view the simplest course was to believe all that the radio, press and posters said about communists and Social Democrats having set fire to the Reichstag. No nation is without a percentage of voters who work on the ebb and flow principle.

EPILOGUE

Statistics[22] of the electoral results from 1930 to 1933 show the following:

ELECTORAL RESULTS 1930-1933

(votes in millions, Reichstag seats in brackets)

	14.9.1930		31.7.1932		6.11.1932		5.3.1933	
Total Electorate	42·97		44·22		44·37		44·69	
Valid Votes	34·97		36·88		35·47		39·34	
Poll Percentage	82%		84%		80·6%		88·7%	
Seats in Reichstag	577		608		584		647	
NSDAP	6·4	(107)	13·77	(230)	11·73	(196)	17·27	(288)
German Nationals	2·45	(41)	2·18	(37)	3·13	(52)	3·13	(52)
German Peoples Party	1·57	(30)	0·43	(37)	0·66	(11)	0·43	(2)
Centre	4·12	(68)	4·58	(75)	4·23	(70)	4·42	(73)
Bavarian Peoples Party	1·05	(19)	1·2	(22)	1·09	(20)	1·07	(19)
Socialist Party	8·57	(143)	7·95	(133)	7·24	(121)	7·18	(120)
Communist Party	4·59	(77)	5·28	(89)	5·98	(100)	4·84	(81)

Analysis of the 5 March 1933 election figures leads to the following:

1. The size of the poll rose by nearly 10 per cent between November 1932 and March 1933. Apart from the NSDAP all parties by and large maintained their vote with the exception of the German Peoples Party which lost 30 per cent. The NSDAP gained about 5·5 million votes and the communists lost some 1·5 million.

2. Valid votes cast rose by about 4 million.

3. Taking together the German Peoples Party and the small parties not shown in the table above (German Landvolk, Christian Social Reich Party, Economic Party, State Party, Peasants Party, Hanoverian Party etc.), their total loss was 1 million votes.

4. Since all the other parties (German Nationals, Centre, Bavarian Peoples Party, Social Democrats) by and large maintained their vote, it follows that the 4 million voters

who did not vote in November 1932 but did so in March 1933 voted for the NSDAP. To these 4 million 'lazybones' were added 1 million deserters who moved over to the NSDAP from the smaller parties of the Centre.

5. Hitler, however, gained 5·5 million, so 500,000 votes still remain to be accounted for. To begin with, some 320,000 new voters were eligible for the March 1933 elections. Considering that they were politically inexperienced youngsters it may be assumed that they were swept along by the brown-shirted current. We should not be far wrong in saying that at least half of them voted National-Socialist. Seeing that, carried away by the Reichstag fire hysteria, some 50,000 Social Democrat supporters sought refuge with the NSDAP, it seems probable that some 200,000-300,000 communist votes also went over. Since, however, the communists polled nearly 6 million in November, this means a loss of barely 5 per cent; it also implies that some 900,000 communist supporters preferred to remain at home – not surprising since they would have been registered by the police at the polling stations and so labelled as having cast their votes for the communist party in spite of the anti-communist campaign. In addition the events connected with the Reichstag fire forced many party functionaries to go underground.

6. These elections proved once more that, with all his organisation and propaganda, Hitler had been unable to influence the national-conservative, Christian, Social Democrat and communist vote. Seeing that one of his main slogans had been that he wished to bring the proletariat back to the nation, this election too was a defeat for him, for of 16 million workers 12 million voted Social Democrat or communist. Since the Christian trade unions voted for the Centre, it follows that at least 13-14 million workers had said 'No' to Hitler.[23] Adding those who were afraid to vote, it appears that Hitler had a bare 10 per cent of the workers behind him. The fact that the NSDAP vote increased by up to 20 per cent in certain working-class areas does not mean that these

were all working-class votes; the areas also included traders, craftsmen, officials and retired people. Once more Hitler's plan to unite nationalism and socialism had not materialised.

This result shed a curious light on elections as a system. Under normal circumstances Hitler would have had to reckon with increased opposition from the Left, sufficient to affect the weight he carried in the coalition government. His aim, of course, was an absolute majority in the Reichstag independent of support from the German Nationals whom he intended to offload as partners as soon as possible. This he achieved by subterfuge. Though he allowed the communists to draw up an electoral list, the arrest of Ernst Thälmann even before 5 March indicated what awaited the party. A communist list was tolerated solely to keep communist votes away from the Socialist party. Once its list had served this purpose, the communist party was banned. The cancellation of the communist seats gave Hitler his absolute majority at one stroke: The 288 NSDAP deputies now formed 51 per cent of the remaining 566 seats (in the original 647 they had only 43·9 per cent). Such was the legal and democratic seizure of power by the NSDAP!

Any objective analysis is bound to reach this devastating conclusion. This is the answer to all the falsifiers of history of various shades of opinion and their speculations about Hitler's 'devilish' power or the German people's tendency to sell themselves to a crude dictator and acclaim his *Götterdämmerung* policy. The fact is that the vast majority of the Christians and the workers never voted for Hitler. The others, who did vote for the NSDAP, were a minority and not all of them regarded Hitler as the saviour; they thought of him rather as the man with whom the 'élite', the German Nationals, had allied themselves and whom they had made Chancellor. What else could the man in the street do when all the most intelligent and courageous had been carted off to concentration camps? The relatives of those taken into protective custody trembled at the very word Gestapo and evinced a certain loyalty towards the régime in the hope of curtailing or at least alleviating the sufferings of their loved ones. Those not so affected were systematically and scientifically brainwashed by Goebbels' propaganda machine. 'Incompetent and criminal' politicians disappeared from public life. The 'best brains' of the Party, the modern miracle men, were continuously praised and fêted. Every one of Hitler's dignitaries had his intelligence and press staff; public opinion everywhere was at the mercy of the Propaganda Ministry and the Secret Service.

When, on 27 February 1933, von Papen saw the Reichstag in flames and Hugenberg heard the news, they realised why Hitler had pressed for elections. The next day they aired their misgivings and asked Göring pointblank whether the communists really had any need to set the Reichstag on fire. Each had suspected that behind Hitler's confidence in the result of the forthcoming elections must lie some fresh propaganda 'miracle'. And the 'miracle' was not long in coming: it consisted of the total subjection of the government machine and of public opinion by means of a *coup d'état*, by means of the false accusation that the Social Democrats and communists had been planning an insurrection. The background to Nazism's victory was crime and deceit; the plebiscite on the Enabling Law held on 24 March 1933 was nothing but the requiem mass following the sentence of death pronounced on 30 January and carried out on 27 February. This victory Hitler owed primarily to Joseph Goebbels, his astute propaganda chief; the Reichstag fireworks had taken the place of the Führer's 'freedom flights'. Goebbels was appointed Reich Minister of Propaganda because with his scenario he had captured 4 million 'lazybones' and 1·5 million renegades.

The day after the fire, while Hitler was laying hands on the propaganda, police and government machines and announcing that the choice in the election was 'Brown or Red', Oberfohren was the first to alert his friends that the

Reichstag fire had been a planned provocation; he had indicated as much in his November speech. At that time, however, he was not to know that the 'closure of the Reichstag' referred to by Goebbels would take the form of actual destruction.

After the Reichstag fire Breiting was able to see both Hugenberg and Oberfohren, and he kept shorthand notes of their discussions. His papers show that Himmler's minions were already intriguing against Oberfohren, so that he went in fear of his life and had to resign as leader of the parliamentary party.[24] Oberfohren possessed detailed information on how Hitler had introduced his puppet van der Lubbe into the Reichstag. He therefore demanded the formation of a Commission of Reichstag members to investigate the background to the fire. In doing so he signed his own death warrant. He was condemned to 'suicide' in the same way as Dr. Erich Klausener, the leader of Catholic Action, who was murdered on 30 June 1934.[25] On 7 May 1933, when his wife was out of the house, Oberfohren was found dead at his desk. Two days later the Kiel registry office certified to Frau Oberfohren that her husband had shot himself. On 4 November 1933 at the Reichstag fire trial Göring stated that Oberfohren had committed suicide because his 'treachery' to Hugenberg, his party leader, had been exposed.[26] Horrifyingly some amateur historians still accept Göring's lying statement even today. Reichstag members like Paul Löbe and historians like Walter Görlitz believe that Oberfohren was assassinated. Breiting's notes show clearly that Oberfohren was a victim of the Reichstag fire plot and that the bullet which killed him was intended as a warning shot to intimidate Hugenberg and others.[27] Frau Doris Bünger, widow of the President of the Leipzig Reich Court, told me that during the Leipzig trial she and her husband went in constant fear of their lives, also that people had tried to intimidate her, that she had received mysterious telephone calls and that detectives had prevented her having any contact with the outside world.

These and others were the methods used in preparation for the electoral victory of 5 March 1933 and the plebiscite of 12 November. Public opinion was coerced by falsehood, deceit and murder.

Hugenberg was forced to resign from the cabinet; von Papen did not remain as Commissar in Prussia for long. Step by step Hitler seized total power. By 30 June 1934 he was strong enough to carry out a bloody purge in his own ranks. On the same day his Reichswehr opponent General von Schleicher was murdered with his friend General von Bredow. Von Papen lost three friends and members of his staff in the same purge.

Some four months earlier, on 6 March 1934 to be exact, Breiting had once more had occasion to see Hitler. On that day Karl-Friedrich Goerdeler, the Burgomaster of Leipzig and a friend of Breiting's, received the Reich Chancellor Adolf Hitler on the occasion of the stone-laying ceremony for the new national Richard Wagner memorial. Frau Winifred Wagner was present and a romantic speech by Hitler turned the Wagner commemorative festivities into a demonstration in honour of all great German artists. Good play-actor that he was, Hitler wept and the *Völkischer Beobachter* wrote: 'The Führer was visibly much affected as he spoke.'

Breiting's notes include the following comment by Goerdeler on Hitler's visit: 'Do not be too pessimistic, my friend. As you saw, the man was almost choking with tears when speaking of poets and art. As I have already told you, he is heart and soul an architect. We will give him every opportunity to be an architect; sooner or later he will be prepared to leave economics and official business to the experts.'

As Burgomaster and Hitler's economics adviser (he was Reich Prices Commissioner for a time) Goerdeler shielded Breiting from political persecution until the latter's death on 28 April 1937. The next day he wrote to Frau Breiting in his own hand praising the dead man's character and his 'valuable advice'.

After some years of the Hitler régime Goerdeler too was forced to admit that the dictator was no artist and was an architect only of death. Goerdeler joined the resistance and was one of the leading figures in the 20 July 1944 conspiracy. On 7 September 1944 he was condemned to death for high treason and executed on 2 February 1945.

Like Goerdeler many members of the élite thought that the National-Socialist Chancellor could be influenced. But Hitler hated people who tried to influence him. He despised senior civil servants, chairmen of large firms, generals, ecclesiastical dignitaries, judges and diplomats. He regarded them as 'grovellers' and 'lickspittles' who would not be prepared to 'die for their masters'.[28] This élite, brought up in the imperial tradition of service, was false and hypocritical, he said, and evaded any responsibility. 'This was the reason for weakness in dealing with obvious vital problems.' Hitler considered these 'grovellers' to be opportunists and concluded that, because of their lack of courage, they should 'never take decisions on vital State problems'. Even during the war he would tolerate only one strategic adviser, General 'Yes-man'. In several passages in *Mein Kampf* Hitler had demanded unconditional subordination to his orders and he had specifically repeated this to Breiting as a *sine qua non*, applicable equally to 'supreme power in the state', the press which Breiting represented, the arts, science, justice, the Wehrmacht and the churches. Having been so clearly warned, what was the élite waiting for?

The élite ought to have sought and found some solution. They might, for instance, have joined forces with the Christians and the marxists to overcome the crisis together and resist the assault of fascist barbarism. But the élite held its tongue and gave Hitler its benevolent support. They hoped that with him they could construct a dictatorship conforming to their own ideas. And that spelt their doom. Unfortunately

135

the people had to pay the bill. From the outset the élite regarded everything left of the bourgeois centre – the Social Democrats and the communists – as enemies. They were therefore pleased when anti-marxists were appointed to important posts. Hitler made use of this attitude to infiltrate his adherents into other parties and, more important still, into the police. By misusing their positions of confidence the Nazi trusties placed in the police and the various parties not only kept Heydrich informed but were also able to intrigue against the republican forces, further the progress of the Nazis and conceal their crimes. As an example, for which documentary evidence exists, of the Nazi's methods of infiltration, a certain Reinhold Heller, an ex-Weimar Republic official, was recommended for a senior police post by Rudolf Diels, the Head of the Gestapo; the recommendation, however, noted that Heller had only joined the 'democratic party' to keep out the marxists and in particular the Social Democrats.[29] As a 'democrat' with an anti-communist label Heller could stab the Weimar Republic in the back without attracting attention. In 1933 he and his colleagues Rudolf Braschwitz, Walter Zirpins and Helmuth Heisig acted as stage managers for the Reichstag fire trial and 'provided' the Public Prosecutor with 170 'witnesses' to enliven Hans Frank's travesty of justice.

Even before the seizure of power the Berlin Criminal Police stood back and took no action against the activities of the 'subordinate staff'. This was an organisation formed by Daluege and Heydrich and led by the notorious SS Commander Herbert Packebusch; it was entrusted with 'special missions' and was the terror of democrats and Jews. The police equally did nothing about Military Intelligence which, on the pretext of national defence, was working as early as 1932 with the 'Specially employed Group Staff', another Heydrich-Daluege invention directed by SS-Gruppenführer Friedrich Wilhelm Krüger. Had these secret organisations not been working together, Hitler could never have staged his provocation. The infiltrators used their cover as members of the 'legality party' to drive Social Democrats and communists out of office as opponents of the future order of society. Their exaggerated anti-communism of course did not mean that they were necessarily serving the Weimar Republic. Files of ex-Gestapo officials found after 1945 show clearly that by 1932 Hitler supporters in the secret service and police were using the underworld to produce 'proof' that the communists were getting money and arms from the Jews in order to fight the National-Socialists.[30]

Hitler laid it down that a statesman or even an official need not be bound by juridical norms. This was the conclusion he drew, not only from his conviction that he was a person of world-historical importance, but also from his contention (totally false) that his political opponents and the Jews were preparing to strike against him and the German people. According to Hitler the brave German soldiers had already once been betrayed by this same 'trash' – when the politicians had 'stabbed them in the back' in 1918. When fighting the Weimar Republic and its representatives, therefore, there were no binding rules of law. It was all a question merely of 'creative capacity' and the right of the stronger. According to the new National-Socialist code of morals, therefore, lying and bloodshed were legitimate methods.

After the Reichstag fire Hitler wished to rid himself of the poor abused human tool, van der Lubbe the 'fire-raiser'; he proposed to have him hanged, saying to his reluctant ministers that he 'did not recognise the doctrine "Law must remain law" when the entire existence of the state was at stake'.[31] Though the remark is recorded only in summary form in the cabinet minutes of 7 March 1933, it shows that basically Hitler considered that officially ordered murder was permissible if it was in the political interest. Hindenburg, however, did not accept this principle and so Hitler was unable to liquidate van der Lubbe straightaway. Only several months later could he rid himself of his unhappy victim by means of a judicial murder.

After his murder of Schleicher, Röhm and the rest on 30 June 1934 Hitler declared that all the crimes he had ordered were legal being 'in emergency defence of the State'.[32] Hans Günther, a senior State attorney, comments: 'The legality principle had been observed once more; everything was perfectly in order; the Reich Minister of Justice knew his positivist legal cole.'[33] Hitler had already expounded to Breiting his principle that 'whatever serves the vital interests of the nation is legal' and he had added that he wished to give the criminal police 'greater discretion' in order to 'increase the State's authority'.

Documents discovered since the war prove that Heydrich and Gestapo Müller had succeeded in transforming the criminal police into an instrument of State policy. Political opponents and Jews were branded as criminals. The loyalty of criminal police and security officials was judged by the energy they showed in persecuting political 'criminals'. Confiscation of property, starvation and bestial murder of Jews became part of 'scientific criminal police procedure'.[34] Alongside these administrative measures the anti-Jewish campaign throughout the country increased in violence.

It may be a historical fact that, when he seized power, Hitler was supported by only a minority of the German people; nevertheless later he did succeed in bringing the majority over to his side. Before the seizure of power the middle class had hoped that Hitler would solve the economic crisis; after 1933 a large part of the working class also fell victim to his trickery. War preparations made it possible to find work once more for all the unemployed; Hitler's 'miracle men' built autobahns for his 'blitz'; every German was to have his Volkswagen. The Führer organised the Winter Help, built houses, arranged factory outings, created the Strength through Joy movement, introduced Labour Service for the young, paid tribute to mothers and children and gave thousands of young men 'their chance' to become officers, telling them that 'two years military service is tantamount to prolonging your life by twenty years'. Every family had its people's radio set bringing Goebbels' voice into every household – and he did not produce abstract theories but spoke of sensational events, the forces of evil invariably planning some attack on the life of the Führer whenever he was engaged in doing something 'great'. The Germans were told that the Spanish Civil War and the French Popular Front were world dangers, that Spanish women and children were being soaked in petrol and burnt. The Condor Legion, which Hitler sent to Spain, was described as an expedition despatched to protect civilisation. Even when firmly in the saddle Hitler still organised a series of major and minor provocations. Having no opportunities of comparison, the masses were turned into intellectual paupers. It is hardly surprising that, under the influence of his spurious egalitarianism and of his propaganda, six million men gave their lives for the country he ruled.

During the Third Reich period German society underwent an enormous change of outlook, not to be erased by a lost war. Structural change was a mere veneer introduced to facilitate the intellectual enslavement of all the various strata – youth, students, workers, peasants, petty bourgeois, intelligentsia, civil servants, military and upper middle class. A mighty society of soldiers and functionaries was formed, allied to monster paramilitary formations; women were forced to work. Taken as a whole this amounted, in fact, to total mobilisation of the people. The ostensible structural changes aroused hopes and acted as a carrot. People no longer wanted egalitarianism but privilege, and that in a heterogeneous society and a continental New Order based on the master-and-slave principle. Recent events have shown that, even in an unjust cause, soldiers will still march into foreign countries and make war. When soldiers do what they believe to be their duty, whether as a matter of discipline or in obedience to the military virtues, it is unjust to blame an entire people and still more several generations of it.

In 1968 the Berlin Court, basing its judgement solely on the Leipzig so-called 'documents', commuted the death sentence on van der Lubbe to one of eight years imprisonment. One can only deplore the fact that it saw fit to add to its 'reasons' the following: 'It is indisputable that Hitler was legally appointed Reich Chancellor. Equally the remarkable increase in votes won by the National-Socialists at elections between 1930 and 1932 shows that a high proportion of the German people placed its trust in Hitler at that time. The Reich Court's statements may be found distasteful and distressing today since they bear humiliating testimony to the political immaturity and lack of instinct of the German people; this does not, however, invalidate them.'[35]

By referring to the 'remarkable increase in votes won by the National-Socialists at elections between 1930 and 1932' the Berlin Court shows that it has forgotten historical facts to which, as a legal body, it should have attributed due weight. As we have seen, between the elections of 31 July 1932 and those of 6 November 1932 Hitler lost two million votes; with the 11·7 million remaining to him prior to his seizure of power he was representing only one quarter of the German electorate.

The so-called principle of legality was used to conceal the technique of the seizure of power; in addition both the personality of Hitler and his aims were presented in a false light. The Breiting conversations show Hitler in his true colours.

Golo Mann has described Hitler's dealings with other people accurately and realistically: 'Not only did he say what seemed most advantageous to say at the time; he actually believed it. Such liars are always the most convincing.' To Breiting as a representative of the bourgeoisie Hitler developed his theories about the state and parliamentarianism, about the rule of law and peace, about Germany's mission on the continent of Europe and England's role in the world. He had no wish to frighten Breiting off with bellicose ideas. He was occupied with plans for the reconstitution of the General Staff and the reorganisation of the Reichswehr, as indeed he indicated in these talks; details of his plans he reserved for another audience, the Generals. Rauschning was given some hint of them. But Rauschning did not record Hitler in shorthand; he merely produced notes from memory, indicating Hitler's warlike intentions. Hitler gave Breiting no more than an indication of his colonisation policy. There was of course no mention of the 'Final Solution of the Jewish Question', though he did refer to expulsion and resettlement of the Jews. The 'Final Solution' could only be entrusted to the 'select', the SS, the deathshead devotees of the mythology of the blood. The Reichsführer's 'Overall Plan for the East' undoubtedly stemmed from a Führer directive.

If a man like Adolf Hitler was determined to implement ideas and plans of this sort and if he had at his disposal a monstrous machine constructed by his 'best brains', small wonder that his time was one of the most gruesome periods of world history. He pursued his strategic fantasies with intuition, energy, a remarkable gift for simplification and organisation, fanaticism and tactical method inspired by determination. Neither in tactics nor strategy did he recognise moral or legal obligations. He ordered crime in order to have himself worshipped as a divine being, well aware that, being in control of the propaganda machine, he could always impute these crimes to his enemies. Hitler was a 'horrific human phenomenon' who conceived and brought into being a gigantic organisation for destruction.

If we are to dismantle this monstrous infernal machine so that it can never again be reconstructed, it is not enough merely to destroy it and congratulate oneself that its master builder is dead. It was, after all, the result of the combined efforts of many people, without whom the master builder would never have been able to construct it. Today the engineers of the construction group maintain that this infernal machine did not in fact possess the qualities attributed to it. To counter them we must be able, theoretically and scientifically, to reconstruct this machine; then we shall be in a position to begin to dismantle it and lay out its component parts. Only then shall we be able to unmask the liars.

We should never forget that Germany's fate was sealed on the day when Hitler swore his legality oath to the Leipzig court. Innumerable malcontents, idealists and dupes regarded Hitler's solemn oath as evidence of his firm determination to defend the basic principles of the Weimar Republic. He appeared as the longed-for reformer. Hitler's most potent slogans with which he deceived a large part of the German people were the 'legality principle' and 'the road which leads to power via the Reichstag'. Had he frankly explained that he proposed to achieve his aims by deception, fire and murder and to make his enemies responsible for these crimes, he would never have been able to consolidate his power. The German people was forced to submit to a brutal dictatorship, not by the Enabling Law of 24 March 1933 but by the accession to power of a schemer and usurper, made possible only by virtue of the emergency clause in the constitution.

This is the lesson which we must draw from history. We should reflect that those great words 'legality' and 'democracy' are frequently no more than a façade behind which criminal ideologies thrive. Our judgement should be based, not upon the vociferousness with which we are assured that legality and democracy are the aims, but on the ideas, emotions and intellectual achievements of 'defenders of justice and civilisation'.

In 1933 Germany fell victim to a commonplace improviser, expert at exploiting favourable circumstances. The country was ruled by a cold-blooded, sophisticated and calculating Machiavelli, who knew how to use intrigue, threats and provocation to create situations necessary to the achievement of his aims; he was also adept at choosing the right allies. Before his seizure of power the National-Socialist leader acted as does the criminal who covers up before committing his crime and, by diversionary manoeuvres, seeks to provide himself with a cast-iron alibi. Once he had become Chancellor, however, he introduced into the state the methods of the underworld. He was convinced that he had no need to render acount of his deeds to anyone at any time. In his conversations with Breiting Hitler revealed himself totally and no one can pretend that his subsequent actions did not tally with his original intentions. From the outset the Führer made no secret of his gangster methods and the rules of the democratic game forbade anyone to ally himself with this representative of a heterogeneous anti-democratic minority.

Despite the unparalleled bestialities practised in Germany by Hitler and his minions, in innumerable ways the German people gave proof of its resistance; representatives abroad kept the flag of German decency flying and in all sections of the population there were those who refused to be blinded by large-scale deception manoeuvres and promises about a Thousand-Year Germanic Reich and took their stand on liberty and humanism. Among those who gave their lives for the brotherhood of nations were workers, bourgeois, Christians, liberals, officers and officials. Their death was very different from that of the street-fighting thugs whom Hitler acclaimed as national heroes and martyrs. Those 'martyrs' were but the outriders for the Four Horsemen of the Apocalypse.

Great souls like Albert Einstein, Thomas Mann and Carl von Ossietzky issued their warnings against this group of conspirators who talked of peace when they meant war and swore oaths to legality when they were planning to destroy all democratic institutions. How far-sighted they were was proved by the symbolic destruction of the Reichstag building, the emergency regulations, the Enabling Law, the engineered plebiscites, the Nuremberg Laws, the special courts, protective custody, Führer decrees – all leading to world war, Auschwitz and unconditional surrender. How was it possible that the politicians of that time could place their trust in men like Hitler, Göring or Goebbels and disregard the warnings of men like Einstein, Mann or von Ossietzky? The 'realist politicians' preferred to see in these professional fascists and their thumping of the nationalist drum the reawakening of a people rather than a deadly danger to the nation.

When St. John in the Revelation described the catastrophes which would overtake the world, his foreboding was of mankind's fate should supreme power fall into the hands of a tyrant. In his day Titus destroyed Jerusalem and his brother Domitian massacred his opponents. Hitler could praise a man like Dürer but would never think of drawing inspiration from the work of the great Nuremberg painter. From the day when he decided to become a politician and a statesman he saw himself as one of the Horsemen of the Apocalypse who swept through the world in the guise of disease, war, starvation and death. He worshipped the power of destruction and it drove him on to use it. Arson, poison, murder and war were the steeds on which he rode into the abyss. There were many St. Johns in Germany who grasped the significance of Dürer's picture; unfortunately they were overborne by those who complacently rode with the sinister horseman on his adventure.

Breiting's shorthand record is a unique document because it sheds the light of truth on Hitler's personality and his aspirations and shows how deliberate and methodical was 'the Führer's muddled thinking'. In his twelve years of power Hitler did, or at least tried to do, everything which he divulged to Breiting. No one can now say that this man was too stupid to think out and implement grandiose plans or that, like Don Quixote, he was so dazzled that he mistook wine-skins for robbers. The only people who now have an interest in presenting Hitler in this light are the technicians who stage-managed the provocations intended to deceive the German people and the world at large. The élite too, who brought him to power by the misuse of their political mandate, may also wish to present him thus for the benefit of coming generations. According to these technicians and politicians there was no Third Reich, no ideology, no domination by force; instead both they and Hitler were the victims of a series of quirks of history which drove the excitable Führer from one extreme to the next. They remained at their posts, they say, in order to avert the worst. This argument we can accept only in the case of those who, in face of Hitler's tyranny, were forced to bow to the realities of life and who, by their resistance, attempted to liberate the German people from the claws of the brown-shirted monster; it cannot be accepted from those whom documents prove to have been on the side of the forces of Satan and who dragged into the mud the honour of the German people.

So the mask is down! Hitler stands revealed as the instigator of all the calamities which he brought upon the German people, the Jews and other nations. A criminal ideology can only be enforced by terror. It can never last.

Hitler revealed the whole range of his plans and intentions only to a few before 1933. To Breiting, however, he unfolded like a panorama all that in his speeches remained concealed behind phrases and gestures, things not even hinted at in *Mein Kampf*, the subterfuges and methods of achieving power, the technique of the legal *coup d'état* to establish total domination over Germany, the brutal extension of his tyranny over all Europe from the Atlantic to the Urals and the megalomaniac vision of world domination. He showed himself with his mask down, yet still with the innermost mask, concealed behind which lay chaos. As the mob acclaimed the Führer, little did it think that it was idolising the incarnation of destruction. Hitler wished to build for himself a monument which would last for centuries. All that remained of him was the blackened skull which the Russians found among the ruins of the Reich Chancellery in May

1945. A people capable of tidying up the heap of ruins into which its country had degenerated, must also be able to find ways and means of rooting out the spiritual debris left by this disastrous past.

It is my hope that by this document the German people, who have bequeathed so many great names to humanism, will be led to the threshold of a new world and so give the lie to all those who, by crying 'Wolf', give the outside world fresh cause for apprehension. May it also encourage all honest Germans to deal ruthlessly with the false prophets. Truth wears no mask and tolerates no distortion.

In concluding this book I would emphasise that I do not for one moment pretend that the Hitler/Breiting conversations automatically revealed all the secrets of contemporary history, still less that my comments represent the *ultima ratio* of historical or sociological argument. This book is no more than an indication, a spur perhaps to further historical research and to the search for the truth. Day by day the truth must be fought for afresh. The battle is forced upon historians of all countries by the writers of legend and the retailers of lies. Unless upon the military victory won among the hecatombs of the battlefields we are determined to build a better future for mankind, we are not worthy to call ourselves victims of National-Socialism – and among these victims I include the six million German dead. We are fighting for the soul, for the heart, of the German people.

NOTES AND COMMENTS

Introduction

1. Breiting was a member of the German Peoples Party. He had numerous politician friends, including Carl-Friedrich Goerdeler, Dr. Wilhelm Bünger and Dr. Ernst Oberfohren.

2. In 1931 the paper reached a circulation of 200,000.

3. On 25 July 1968 Dr. Alfred Detig, an ex-member of the *Leipziger Neueste Nachrichten* editorial staff, who had been present at the first Hitler-Breiting interview, told me that Hitler's intention had been to blackmail him and Breiting and force them into compliance with his policy and membership of his party. He also stated that the meeting had been arranged by Otto Dietrich, Hitler's press adviser. Dietrich, however, was not present at the talks. After 1933 Max Amann, Hitler's Company Sergeant-Major in the First World War, head of the Party publishing firm Franz Eher II from 1922 and finally President of the Reich Press Chamber, managed to gain control of the newspaper.

4. In his talks with Breiting Hitler assured him that he had in his movement the 'best brains' in Germany as experts on various problems; he also spoke of justice, law and a new order in Europe. It is therefore worth giving some details about Dr. Hans Frank, his legal adviser. Frank had been a friend of Feder, Hitler's economic adviser, ever since 1919 and was a committed National-Socialist from the outset. He took part in the 1923 *putsch* as an SA despatch rider. In 1927 he became a barrister in Munich and a year later formed the National-Socialist Lawyers Association. In 1929 Hitler made him head of the Legal Bureau in Party Headquarters. He represented Hitler at the trial of three National-Socialist officers in Ulm in 1930 and in the same year became a Reichstag deputy. After the seizure of power he rose rapidly, becoming Minister of Justice in Bavaria. He founded the 'German Legal Front' and in 1933 the 'Academy for German Law' of which he was President. He unified the legal system throughout the *Länder*. In his view the existing system was 'byzantine in origin and partially governed by a Jewish spirit'; it should be replaced by a system of 'German law'. What he meant by this, however, was shown by the 'Reichstag Fire Trial', a judicial farce staged under his direction before the Leipzig Reich Court, also by the notorious principle enunciated at the 1935 anniversary of the foundation of the 'Academy': 'Love for the Führer has become a legal concept.' Hitler created him Minister of the

Reich and later Governor of occupied Poland. As a coloniser Frank invented the famous slogan: 'Only master-race types can lead the East.' In 1946 he was condemned to death by the Nuremberg Tribunal and executed.

First Interview

1. Like Breiting, Detig was also a member of the German Peoples Party.

2. It was no accident that this figure of Christ was placed alongside the golden swastika. In all his political dealings Hitler made logical and sophisticated use of the stick and carrot method. He and his entire entourage let it be known that they were basically anti-Christian; nevertheless Hitler attempted to win the church over to his policy by a series of false promises. After 1933, despite the assurances which he had given the Catholic Church, he had no hesitation in using threats and provocation against its leading members to force them to go along with him. His method was to assure himself of an unassailable political alibi by giving his personal agreement in certain credible cases. At the same time, however, he arranged for his subordinates to take the severest possible measures. On Hitler's chicanery towards Christianity and the Churches see Note 35 (p. 158).

3. The fittings of the 'Brown House' and its vast administrative machine show that, even in 1931, the NSDAP could call upon considerable resources. Emissaries paid regular visits to industrial and financial personalities in order to keep the Party coffers filled. Fritz Thyssen and his friends were supporting Hitler's movement long before 1933. After the seizure of power certain industrialists and bankers formed an association known as the 'Friends of the Riechsführer-SS Heinrich Himmler'.

4. Frederick II (The Great), 1712-1786, the embodiment of Prussianism.

5. Hitler was quite content to leave Breiting, as representing the bourgeoisie and conservative Saxon circles, with the impression that the National-Socialists were irresistibly on the move to victory. The agitator was not even interested in the publication of the interview in the press. Instead he wished to win Breiting over and he knew what a brain-washing exercise this would entail. He had to be careful that his ideas did not alert his internal and external enemies. He therefore wished to avoid publication of his statements at all costs. He proposed to continue to throw dust in the eyes of the world. At this point his requirement was to attract disciples and win over the manipulators of the influential press. With apparent total lack of concern he refused a press interview in order to save the paper from

loss of advertisement custom. Three years later, however, Richard Breiting had to swallow the accusation that he was a lackey of the Jews for accepting advertisements from Jewish firms. Knowing (and despising) Breiting's old-fashioned notions of honour, Hitler bound him to secrecy, confident that he would keep his promise. Hitler himself, however, never felt bound by his own word. On 26 February 1932 he swore allegiance to the Weimar constitution and on 30 January 1933 announced that he wished to rule in a parliamentary manner. In fact, however, he engineered a series of provocations in order to justify his extra-constitutional claims to power.

6. It should be emphasised that Hitler refers here to a turning point, not only for Germany but for the whole of Europe. He foresaw that his alternative, bolshevism or National-Socialism, would drive the right-wing parties into his arms. But just as he proposed to confront the German nationalists with this choice, he also wished to force the conservative forces in Europe, particularly in England, to opt for him.

7. Hitler would not concede that the bourgeois politicians possessed any statecraft. He recognised neither Rathenau nor Stresemann. They lacked that brutality of which he possessed more than enough.

8. After the seizure of power Hitler's insistence on the simple mode of life of the Nazi dignitaries was belied by the facts. Although at the cabinet meeting of 28 February 1933 he promised that the damage to the Reichstag building would be fully repaired, he left it as a ruin and instead constructed an ostentatious new Reich Chancellery with a lavish expenditure of granite and marble. While Hitler was congratulating himself for Breiting's benefit on his modest circumstances, he had ever since 1925 been the owner of a luxuriously furnished country house in Berchtesgaden, 'Haus Wachenfels'. He gave out that the owner was his half-sister Angela Raubal, whose daughter Geli became his mistress. In 1935 he enlarged this property and had the spacious 'Berghof' built. His new mistress, Eva Braun, had a whole floor and a swimming pool at her disposal. Little gazebos were installed on the mountain tops and lifts carved out of the cliffs. With this Berchtesgaden 'Sanssouci' and his large well-appointed apartment in the Prinzregentenstrasse Munich, he could well afford to dispense with a villa in Travemünde or Switzerland. All the Third Reich dignitaries had town houses, country estates and hunting lodges; the 'modest' Reichsführer-SS Himmler, for instance, had a villa in a smart quarter of Berlin where he was attended by fourteen slaves, a hunting lodge north of Berlin, a villa on the Starnberger See and a secret hide-out for his mistress. Göring's profligate mode of life hardly needs mention. Many references are to be found in the Nuremberg Trial to the theft of valuable

paintings from the museums of Europe for the oligarchs' private collections. Hitler himself appropriated some 600 of the most valuable pictures.

9. On 23 March 1933 Hitler repeated this accusation against the Social Democrats when addressing the assembled Reichstag in the Kroll Opera House, a meeting which Göring called the hour of reckoning with liars and traitors. Hitler does not mention the fact that, ever since becoming leader of the NSDAP, he had been hurling curses at the heads of his opponents. Without a shadow of proof he labelled all politicians as criminals and traitors. On the other hand he frequently paid tributes to thugs and murderers. On 23 August 1932, for instance, he sent a message of encouragement to five National-Socialist 'comrades' who had been condemned to death by a special court in Beuthen for breaking into the house of a Pole named Pietrcuch and murdering him before his mother's eyes.

10. Hitler attempted to counter the well-founded accusation that he was an instigator of anarchy by presenting himself as the founder of a new order. In those crisis years the word 'order' was extraordinarily alluring, particularly when the general public did not know what Hitler's plans were for bringing this new order about. As a result of his draconian measures calm ostensibly reigned in Germany after 1933 and, owing to the Nazi control of the information media, the people were largely unaware of the other side of the coin. Even foreign observers were impressed by this regimented order and unity, and by the deceptive economic 'recovery' – all brilliantly advertised at the 1936 Olympics. The false picture has not quite faded even yet; so let us look at the facts.

Hitler's 'order' was introduced and maintained by the Reichssicherheitshauptamt [Reich Central Security Department], Section IV of which was the Gestapo, by a colossal network of informers, by total control of press and radio, by arbitrary arrests, rigged trials and bestial tortures in the concentration camps where by the end of the war and in Germany alone 750,000 political prisoners were confined without trial. To these Himmler added 6,000 'professional criminals' to keep 'order' in the camps. 'Biological hygiene' was ensured by the gas chambers. And all this took place, not in camps outside Germany as people often wrongly maintain, but in Sachsenhausen, Neuengamme, Dachau, Mauthausen and Grossrosen.

11. In a speech to industrialists on 27 January 1932, exactly a year before the Reichstag Fire, Hitler insisted on the right to provocation. He regarded it as a sacred duty, he said, to engineer provocations in order to rouse the masses. Emotion was the decisive driving force of the masses (*Mein Kampf* – Murphy's translation, p. 283). The method employed was of no consequence. The only criterion was furtherance of the NSDAP's interests and of his own

authority. Those who participated in these affairs with energy and enthusiasm or who fell were classified as heroes. The most despicable murderers and their crimes were acclaimed. When the Special Court in Beuthen condemned five National-Socialists to death for murdering Pietrcuch (see Note 9), Hitler sent them a telegram calling them 'my comrades'. When Hitler changed the 'Day of National Mourning' into 'Heroes Day' on 27 February 1934, the anniversary of the Reichstag fire, he placed street thugs and murderers on a level with the war dead. 'Heroes Day' was celebrated on the fifth Sunday before Easter. It is characteristic of Hitler that he promulgated the law on the anniversary of the Reichstag fire.

12. Later General Ludwig Beck, appointed Chief of Staff of the Army by Hitler in 1935. Beck resigned in 1938 and was subsequently one of the 20 July 1944 conspirators. Beck, who was a Colonel at the time, was highly critical of the arrest by the police of Lieutenant Wendt and 2nd Lieutenants Scheringer and Ludin. These three officers were in the dock at the so-called 'Ulm Trial' in 1930 for forming secret Nazi groups in their units. As a result of this criticism Hitler concluded that Beck approved of his Reichswehr policy.

13. In 1918 Wilhelm Groener (1867-1939) was Deputy Chief of Staff I in Army Headquarters. He became Reich Minister of Transport in 1920, Reichswehr Minister in 1928 and Minister of the Interior in 1931. Hitler knew that he could expect nothing from Groener and his friends. Nevertheless when the Centre and Social Democrats proposed a motion to extend Hindenburg's period in office, a measure requiring a two-thirds majority in the Reichstag, and the Reichswehr Minister was trying to persuade the Nazi deputies to support it, Hitler negotiated with Groener. Though conducted 'in friendly fashion', the talks were fruitless. Hitler had his own ideas on who should be the next Reich President and how he should be elected.

Hitler regarded General Kurt Schleicher (1882-1934), the political head of the Reichswehr, as a dangerous opponent and competitor. In 1929 Schleicher became State Secretary in the Reichswehr Ministry and as Head of the Ministerial Office dealt with both the internal and external political problems of the Reich. He built up his own information service and allied himself to the aristocracy and their adherents. He was a friend of Crown Prince Wilhelm. Early in January 1932 Hitler and Schleicher met for a secret discussion and the General was deluded into thinking that Hitler would accept a two-thirds majority for the extension of Hindenburg's Presidency. In fact, however, Hitler thought that the fifty-year-old General, who was in high favour with Hindenburg, had designs on a political career himself. Hitler refused Schleicher's proposal, repeated later by Groener and Brüning, for 'constitutional,

UNMASKED

internal and external political, and moral reasons'. He wished to be a candidate himself. In 1932 Schleicher was appointed Reichswehr Minister and from 2 December 1932 to Hitler's seizure of power he was Reich Chancellor. In this position he thought that he could turn some of Hitler's associates into allies; in addition, together with Gregor Strasser and his adherents, he hoped to split the NSDAP. He worked out various plans to deal with the crisis and stop the rise of National-Socialism. His entire effort was concentrated on countering Hitler's claim to power and preventing him fulfilling his ambition to become Head of State and Supreme Commander of the Army. Schleicher had to pay for his opposition with his life; on 30 June 1934 Hitler had the General and his wife murdered together with General von Bredow.

14. The so-called martyrs list with its 300 names was a great exaggeration. Hitler in fact labelled as a 'martyr of the movement' anyone who had belonged to the SA or SS, been involved in some brawl and been killed in the process. To make the list more imposing, he included the names of underworld figures who had met their fate as 'vigilantes' for the police and SD. Far more people had been murdered by the Nazis before the seizure of power. In an interview which Hitler gave to the *Rheinisch-Westfälische Zeitung* on 16 August 1932 he was still insisting on this figure of 300; he admitted, however, that during 1931 the number of wounded had reached 6,000 and that 8,200 had been hurt during the first $7\frac{1}{2}$ months of 1932 (*Völkischer Beobachter*, 17 August 1932). Official NSDAP figures of 15 August 1932 show a total of 192 'martyrs'. When Hitler was speaking to Breiting the number was about 100. The Führer apparently felt justified in multiplying by three. In any case these figures are eloquent proof of the terror spread in the streets by his mobile squads.

15. As it turned out Hitler's forecast was correct. On 20 July 1932 by virtue of Article 48 of the Weimar Constitution ('for the re-establishment of public law and order') Hindenburg authorised von Papen, the Chancellor, in his capacity as Reich Commissar for Prussia, to relieve the Prussian Ministers of their offices. Lieutenant-General von Rundstedt, commanding the Army Group Headquarters I, was commissioned to use Reichswehr officers to dismiss Otto Braun, the Prussian Minister-President, Carl Severing, the Minister of the Interior, and Albert Grzesinski, the Police President.

16. Here Hitler is referring to the revolution of November 1918 which led to the proclamation of the Republic. When he appeared as a witness before the Leipzig Court at the 'Ulm Trial' in 1930, he called the Social Democrats 'November criminals'. He promised that 'heads would roll' on the day when he assumed power. Hitler thereby introduced a criminal connotation into the political stab-in-the-back legend. Shortly after the November 1918 armistice the Generals

152

spread the rumour that they had been forced to urge the Kaiser to end the war because of the munitions strike a month before. Documentary proof exists, however, that on 29 September 1918, in other words before the October strike, Hindenburg and Ludendorff had submitted an urgent request to the Kaiser to conclude an armistice within 48 hours, otherwise the front would collapse. They had decided on this step after having already declared on 14 August that continuance of the war was 'hopeless' and they realised that armistice negotiations must begin before the collapse became total. After the collapse of the Salonika front and the capitulation of Bulgaria the German General Staff knew that Marshal Franchet d'Esperey, the French Commanding General in the South-East, could march on Budapest, Vienna and Prague practically unopposed. The Intelligence Service knew the state of morale in the Austro-Hungarian monarchy. The Alllies might even advance from Italy. The Court camarilla and the Generals seized the opportunity of Hindenburg's and Ludendorff's request for an armistice to install a new government under Prince Max of Baden. It included both the Social Democrats and the Centre Party, a manoeuvre to save the monarchy, prevent revolution and shift responsibility for the loss of the war on to the politicians. They and the Reichstag were to be responsible for the armistice, not the military or the Kaiser who had hitherto called the tune. When Ludendorff realised that he would have no post-war role to play and that the Kaiser was prepared to sacrifice him, he decided on 24 October to let the army fight on. He had not of course suddenly become convinced that the front could hold; he wished to emerge as the strong man and made use of the demands meanwhile formulated in the exchange of notes as a pretext for his obduracy. This phase ended with his dismissal on 26 October and the Austrian request for an armistice on 27 October. When the representatives of the Reichstag then signed the armistice, Ludendorff and his officers screamed 'treachery'. Their claim that, for the sake of honour, all should have been staked on one last battle was as senseless as the supposition that the outcome of the Second World War would have been more favourable to Germany had Hitler been able to use the last German divisions in the battle for Berlin. From his conversations with Ludendorff Hitler knew that the war had in fact been decided in 1914 when the German Army's initial assault failed to reach Paris and capture the French capital. Germany could never produce the men and equipment at the front to equal the armies of the Entente. Hitler was well aware of the real reasons when he assured Breiting that he had no intention of repeating these mistakes and involving Germany in a war on two fronts.

17. Hitler's statements show clearly that he was looking to his paramilitary formations to bring about a landslide and that his preparations were aimed in two directions: 1. The battle against

communism. 2. The capture as future allies of the conservatives and industry. He never wavered in this purpose until Hindenburg and industry handed power over to him.

18. 'World Jewry's conspiracy' with bolshevism was one of Hitler's pretexts for tarring with the same brush the bourgeois parliamentary system with its 'lack of principle' and the communist movement. Over-simplification and falsehood are the weapons of any agitator. The 'Jewish problem', the 'bolshevist danger', the Social Democrat 'treachery', the 'incompetence' of the bourgeoisie and other slogans were mere rhetorical methods of substantiating his internal and external political aims and his claim to power. His criterion for any problem was whether it was 'expedient' and 'ripe'; he liked to solve things by stages. He would have preferred to begin with the 'Jewish problem', but the German people would not have understood nor the outside world approved. So he decided to start by using the Jews as scapegoats and hostages. Hitler never believed in the existence of some secret Jewish world régime Had there been one he would have dealt with the so-called Jewish problem differently. Like many other problems, Hitler raised these questions in order to inspire the masses both at home and abroad with hatred. His own inspiration he drew from the anti-semitic campaigns and old-fashioned pogroms of the Middle Ages and the previous century. His racial mania was such that he tried to make allies of the Christians by pointing out to them that, after all, it was the Jews who had nailed Christ to the Cross. Expulsion of Jews, anti-Jewish reprisals and the ghettos of the past were measures all too lenient in his eyes. Hitler wished to deal with the Jewish problem (which in fact did not exist) in a novel way. He used the fake *Protocols of Zion*, published in 1924 in Leipzig and in 1932 in Munich (by the Franz Eher concern) as proof of the so-called world Jewish conspiracy. Anyone who did not agree with him in this was labelled as a Jewish minion. But this was mere demagogic pressure to support his own bid for power. Once he had it, he organised the 'Jewish boycott' on 1 April 1933; this he presented as an answer to 'foreign atrocity propaganda' which had accused him and Göring of being the Reichstag fire-raisers and attacked the tortures to which those arrested on the night of the fire had been subjected. Hitler had already designated as the fire-raisers three Jews and Ernst Thälmann, the leader of the communist party; he had planned a second trial to follow that of Dimitroff, Torgler, Popoff, Taneff and van der Lubbe. Public opinion, however, forced him to release four of the five accused and the planned Jewish-communist trial was shelved. As early as 1933 Hitler realised that preparations for the persecution of the Jews must be longer term. The press, radio, cinema and literature were harnessed to the campaign of vilification. The Criminal Police became an instrument for establishing the

criminality of Jewish citizens and their 'minions'. These 'revelations' were disseminated by every conceivable method of propaganda. Anti-semitism eventually became a science. As a result of this chicanery, by 1935 Hitler felt himself strong enough to issue the 'Nuremberg Laws'. These were followed in 1938 by 'Kristallnacht' and in January 1942 the 'Final Solution' began with the Wannsee Conference. The murder squads, in which the élite were blooded, and the gas chambers were the culmination of a long-prepared programme of Jewish persecution announced in *Mein Kampf*. Politically, however, the whole process was so 'inexpedient' that Hitler had it carried out in secret and by the faithful only; to the people it was camouflaged as 'resettlement in the Eastern territories'.

19. The common front with the German Nationalists to which Hitler refers here was formed four months later as the 'Harzburg Front'.

20. The 'November betrayal' was one of Hitler's favourite phrases. In using it he was following the advice of Goebbels who maintained that constant repetition was the first rule of propaganda. This continuous repetition of lies and falsifications of history frequently leads today to the erroneous conclusion that Hitler was the victim of an *idée fixe* and that allowances should therefore be made for him and his gang.

21. Here Hitler speaks quite openly of closing the doors of the Reichstag and erecting some monument alongside it. In fact, after seizing power, he did commission his architect friend Albert Speer to erect a victory arch to the reawakened nation. It was to be on the Königsplatz in front of the Reichstag. Hitler never had the Reichstag rebuilt. On the other hand he commissioned Speer to redesign the Party Rally stadium in Nuremberg in monumental style. At the Nuremberg Rallies Hitler would announce important decisions – the notorious 'Nuremberg Laws' for 'Protection of German blood and honour' in 1935, for instance. The Gauleiter and deputies were merely expected to applaud his pronouncements with a 'Sieg Heil'.

22. The 'better system' consisted of sheer tyranny – no freedom of expression, frontiers closed, rapid though concealed depreciation of the currency, persecution of political opponents and Jews, discrimination against ecclesiastical dignitaries and members of the Reichswehr, introduction of universal military service, concentration camps, provocation of other nations, forged currency, formation of Fifth Columns. All these were the precursors of total war with its mass deportations and scientific preparation for genocide. Yet Hitler had never received such a mandate from the German people. Had he explained at the outset what his 'better system' meant, the NSDAP would never have been supported by 30 per cent of the electorate, the maximum figure it achieved before the Reich-

stag fire despite the economic crisis and Hitler's extravagant demagogy.

23. Hitler frequently maintained that the success of any policy depended on the degree of fanaticism of the masses. He treated the people like a vast munitions factory. First he stockpiled his ammunition and then sent it to the front. Once he had inspired his people with hate, he could loose them on the enemy in the name of his 'higher ethic'. The first essentials for this psychological warfare were the 'Gleichschaltung' of the press, a monopoly of the radio and misuse of the governmental machine for his campaign of discrimination against his enemies. This was no totalitarian discovery made by Hitler after his seizure of power. He had dealt with the subject before the assembled industrialists in Düsseldorf on 27 February 1932 when he had said that the success of a policy depended on the faith of the people and its 'inherent forces'. Neither internal nor external policy could be successfully pursued without these 'forces inherent in faith' – in other words hate. Hitler's expertise in this field is proved by the fact that he was able to drag the German people into the abyss in 1945. It is therefore contrary to all reason when some people say today that those who wished to eliminate the Hitler régime and bring the war to an end were guilty of stabbing in the back the German soldier fighting at the front.

24. Hitler is here openly paying tribute to his closest adviser, Dr. Goebbels, and warning the German intelligentsia that he had every intention of sticking to him. Hitler made Goebbels the Gauleiter of Berlin, not only because he trusted him but because he thought that he could convert the capital to National-Socialism – which in fact he did not do.

25. On 13 March 1933, one week after the successful elections of 5 March when the Nazis won 17 million votes, Hitler announced that he had set up a Reich Ministry of Popular Enlightenment and Propaganda. The newly-appointed Minister was named Dr. Joseph Goebbels, in future to be dictator of the press, radio, theatre, cinema and foreign propaganda.

26. Hitler never carried out his programmed nationalisation of industry. His socialistic phrases were designed only to win over some part of the working class. The left-wing group under Gregor Strasser, which supported nationalisation, was among the victims of 30 June 1934, the 'Night of the Long Knives'.

27. This was a hint by Hitler that he would only too willingly accept a subsidy from industry in order to found a political school for his agitators. Himmler, as head of the secret service, was commissioned to canvass the bourgeoisie, finance and industry for contributions to cover the Party's expenses or 'the suppression of bolshevism', as it was put.

28. In 1925 Hitler renounced his Austrian nationality to avoid

expulsion as an undesirable alien. In his talk with Breiting he laid great stress on the fact that certain influential newspapers had been campaigning for his naturalisation. He became a German citizen in February 1932.

29. The *Leipziger Neueste Nachrichten* had repeatedly demanded that the 'national forces' should seek an understanding with Hitler. Industry and finance both in Saxony and Thuringia were also ardent supporters. Wilhelm Bünger, ex-Minister-President of Saxony and a close friend of Breiting, was among those opposed to any alliance between the Nationalists and the marxists.

30. Here Hitler says that, although he proposed to eliminate the Jews as a cultural and financial grouping, he had no intention of annihilating them on biological grounds. Nevertheless on 1 April 1933, two months after the seizure of power, he organised the first anti-Jewish boycott and later introduced the racist Nuremberg Laws. The Jews may not have been nailed to telegraph poles but they were driven into gas chambers.

31. Dr. Alfred Hugenberg (1865-1951) had been Chairman of the German Nationalist Peoples Party since 1928. He owned certain right-wing and nationalist newspapers and the Ufa film concern. He was opposed to any coalition with the Social Democrats or the Centre. Being a representative of big business with considerable influence on public opinion through the press and cinema, he was a key figure in Hitler's plans. Hitler knew that the German Nationalists had no wish to be associated with the democratic parties in over-coming the crisis. They wished to allow the Social Democrats and Centre to ruin the State by bad management and then sooner or later take it over themselves. It was vital to Hitler to prevent any alliance between the Nationalists and the Centre. To this end he assured the Nationalists that they would be primarily responsible for saving Germany from catastrophe and that his part would be to win the proletariat over to the national coalition. Certain of the leading German Nationalists were only too pleased to see Hitler address himself to the task of detaching the mass of the people from the Left. Secretly they were convinced that, when the time came, they would be able to relegate 'the Corporal' to the rear rank.

32. Dr. Otto Hugo was legal adviser to the Bochum Chamber of Industry and Commerce. He had been a member of the Reichstag since 1920 and was an influential member of the German Peoples Party.

33. Here Hitler is unmistakably announcing his programme for the seizure of power – elimination of the 'talking shop' (the Reichstag), change of attitude on the part of the press, ruthless showdown with Social Democrats and communists. On 27 February 1933 the Reichstag was set on fire, the greater part of the press was banned and the communists and Social Democrats persecuted. All this

occurred 21 months after his interview with Breiting.

34. This also took place according to programme. Nine, not six, months after seizing power Hitler organised the plebiscite of 12 November 1933 when he received a 95 per cent vote. Thus he took his revenge for 8 November 1923 when his *putsch* had miscarried.

35. What did Hitler mean by the words 'the best forces of Christianity?' Before the seizure of power he promised to conclude a concordat; once he was Chancellor, however, he organised rigged trials of ecclesiastical dignitaries and had Dr. Eric Klausener, head of Catholic Action in Berlin, shot. He supported the 'German Christians' and their Reich Bishop, Müller; he persecuted the 'believing church' and consigned Pastors Niemöller and Grüber to concentration camps because their interpretations of the Word of God differed from his own. The 'German mode of life, German ethics and morals' are catch phrases used to conceal his barbaric methods. The word euthanasia was used for the murder of helpless children and sick people; Hitler regarded it as 'mercy killing'. To justify arbitrary persecution, arrests and executions, his opponents were accused of various crimes and discredited by the security agencies and the courts. So there grew up a body of legislation repugnant to the customs, ethics or morals of any people, the German included. A new aristocracy arose which taught the German people 'the necessity for freedom from moral restraints'. Foremost in this programme was the SS, whose members might not belong to any church. In the first phase of the spiritual reformation of the German people they were the privileged caste, the 'believers in God' – but the God they believed in and to whom they swore loyalty was Adolf Hitler. This formed the justification for the extermination of other peoples and races and of the enemy at home, also for the measures of racial hygiene designed to reinforce Germany's biological potential preparatory to the total Germanisation of the continent.

36. Hitler was well aware that his talk of 'socialism' was deceptive. Later in the interview he admitted quite openly that he despised the masses and that 'socialism' was mere demagogy. When with 'respectable' (in other words conservative) people he would admit that he had no intention of introducing socialism. On 1 May 1935, the 'Day of German Labour', he screamed to $1\frac{1}{2}$ million men assembled on Tempelhof airfield: 'Even were I presented with great areas of the world, I would rather be among the poorest of our own folk.' In his talk with Breiting he admitted that he needed capitalism if he was to rearm Germany and give her a position of power in the world. He assured the Tempelhof crowd, however, that the laurels of war had no attraction for him – 'I can only say that my ambition is directed towards triumphs of a different sort'. He promised to erect no memorial to himself; his memorial for future

generations was to be 'the most beautiful stadiums, roads and cities'. The stadiums were designed as parade-grounds for his formations, the autobahns made his armies mobile, other nations' cities served as targets for his attacks. In 1939 Hitler used the Gleiwitz 'provocation' as justification for the invasion of Poland; this was how he made the people and the army 'ripe' for his plans. In spite of his promise he did leave a memorial behind him – the ruins into which he had turned the cities of Germany.

37. Although Knut Hamsun, the 1920 Nobel Prize winner, was a National-Socialist sympathiser, there is no proof that he ever gave vent to ideas such as this. It is interesting to note that Hitler seemed to visualise the destruction of all European parliaments.

38. Here Hitler indicates that he proposes to do away with all buildings housing professional parliamentarians and abolish their institutions – like Constantine who destroyed all idols to guarantee the victory of Christendom.

39. Immediately on seizing power Hitler demanded the dissolution of Parliament. By means of the Reichstag fire he extracted from Hindenburg the 'Ordinance for the Protection of People and State' of 28 February 1933. On 24 March 1933 he forced the Enabling Law through the Reichstag.

40. Hitler is probably referring here to his unhappy experiences of 1923 with Gustav von Kahr, the Bavarian Commissar-General, and his friends. It was due to Kahr and von Lossow that the November *putsch* failed.

41. Otto Strasser was the brother of Gregor Strasser, the Party ideologist. He left the NSDAP in 1930 and openly challenged Hitler.

42. Although Breiting's shorthand refers to Hitler's shining black eyes, Hitler's eyes were in fact blue-grey, as everyone knows. The enlargement of the pupils as seen through Breiting's thick spectacles may account for this mistake.

Second Interview

1. The first wave of arrests took place immediately after the Reichstag fire. That very night Hitler had some 5,000 of his opponents arrested throughout Germany, 1,200 of them in Berlin alone. After Hitler's *coup d'état* there was no further question of regular judicial proceedings against opposition leaders. Hundreds of thousands of Germans remained victims of this arbitrary action right up to 1945. The mere words 'protective custody' and 'concentration camp' were enough to intimidate the ordinary man. Hitler did engineer a real St. Bartholomew's Night on 30 June 1934 – against his own people (the 'Röhm *putsch*').

2. In 1913 Philipp Stauff wrote an anti-semitic pamphlet entitled 'Semi-Kürschner' (Wolf in sheep's clothing).

3. These ideas are to be found in Heinrich Heine's *L'Allemagne* (Paris 1934).

4. Hess had at one time been assistant to the well-known Professor Karl Haushofer, one of the great names of German geopolitics. He saw the future of mankind in a condominium of the Germans and the British over the strategic areas of the world.

5. Dietrich Eckart was the first editor of the *Völkischer Beobachter*, the official newspaper of the Nazi Party. He died in 1923.

6. When he took over power on 30 January 1933 Hitler was prepared to make do with only three ministerial posts for his Party. A few days later he renounced his salary and let it be known that he proposed to live off the royalties from his literary activities. *Mein Kampf*, his first book, brought him in millions of marks.

7. The Conservative Peoples Party was the title of a group led by Gottfried Reinhold Treviranus, Minister of Transport in the Brüning cabinet, which openly opposed National-Socialist policy. Treviranus left the German Nationalist Party in 1928 when Hugenberg was elected as its president. He and his friends thereupon formed their own party. Treviranus was on the black list for the 'Night of the Long Knives' on 30 June 1934 but managed to escape abroad. Hitler never forgave him for his opposition. His name, together with those of Eduard Benesh, the exiled Czechoslovak President, and Lord Vansittart, was mentioned in the communiqué on the 'Bürgerbräu assassination attempt', the provocation engineered to spark off the offensive in the West. All three men were accused of having organised and financed the attempt through the British Secret Service.

8. In fact the number of unemployed reached 5·6 million. Of these 4,713,000 were on national assistance and 244,000 on short time.

9. Either Hitler is at fault here or Breiting made a mistake in his shorthand. The total electorate in the Berlin constituency (Berlin 2) was 1,522,922. On 14 September 1930 the Social Democrats scored 346,019 and the communists 408,626. Either Hitler included Potsdam 1 or Potsdam 2 in his figures in order to swell the number of marxist votes or Breiting omitted to note that Hitler had included areas around Berlin. It is also possible that either Hitler or Breiting got their arithmetic wrong. In Berlin including Potsdam 1 and 2 the Social Democrats and communists combined registered 1·8 million votes, in Berlin with Potsdam 1 alone 1·4 million. Probably this was what Hitler was referring to and he rounded the figure up to 1·5 million. It is worth noting that, taking all three constituencies together, 1·8 million votes went to the marxists and only 0·5 million to the NSDAP. It was therefore correct to say that in the Berlin

constituency the Social Democrats and communists had an absolute majority.

10. This happened on 30 April 1931.

11. In 1937 Hitler appointed his friend Albert Speer General Architectural Inspector and commissioned him to redesign Berlin. By 1943 Max Amann, the head of the National-Socialist press and publishing firm, was controlling up to 80 per cent of the German press.

12. They were used in the service of the Party. Books were burnt, 'degenerate' works of art banished from the museums or sold abroad. All cultural, artistic and scientific contacts with other countries were stopped. Hitler in fact put into practice the ideas he had gathered from Philipp Stauff's pamphlet 'Semi-Kürschner'.

13. Twenty months after this interview Hitler decided to evict the Prussian Academy of Arts from its great building at No. 8 Prinz-Albrecht-Strasse. At his behest the house was made available to the Gestapo as its central headquarters.

14. The Reichstag building was named the Wallot Palace after its architect Paul Wallot. In *Mein Kampf* Hitler referred to it as the meeting place of 'blockheads'.

15. It is remarkable that, as early as this, Hitler should refer to the burning of the Reichstag which he engineered two years later. As early as March 1932 destruction of the parliament building figured on the Nazis' electoral programme. Walter Gempp, the head of the Berlin Fire Brigade, had in his files a poster printed by Goebbels for the Presidential elections showing the Reichstag and its main meeting hall on fire. The inscription was 'It's burning ...' Certain criminal police officers involved in the Reichstag Fire Trial quoted Dr. Ernst Hanfstaengl as a witness to Hitler's astonishment over the fire. On 6 August 1968, however, Hanfstaengl told me that in 1923, in his capacity as Hitler's press adviser, he had attended a meeting when Hitler had said to General von Seeckt: 'The sooner this talking shop is burnt down, the quicker we shall be able to form a new Wehrmacht and new General Staff.'

16. Hitler in fact never did set foot in the 'abode of traitors'. When he visited the Reichstag building on the evening of 27 February 1933 it was already in flames – a spectacle he wished to see.

17. Hitler decided on the building of the autobahns in 1934, soon after his seizure of power. The reconstruction of cities was laid down by law.

18. These plans were financed by raising the fiduciary issue, rationing of raw materials and control of exports and imports. As a result the depreciation of the currency was concealed internally. During the early days of his régime these methods enabled Hitler to keep the currency more or less stable. His principle 'hard work,

low wages, limited purchasing power' was supported by every known device such as the restriction of money circulation by 'severe saving', but even this could not establish a reasonable balance between money circulation and production. The currency lost value and the black market boomed. Draconian measures – imprisonment or even death – were decreed as punishment for rationing abuses in the hope of maintaining some value for the currency.

19. Hitler invariably knew how to turn to his own advantage the moral obligations undertaken by his opponents both at home and abroad. In April 1928 Kellogg, the American Secretary of State, proposed a pact outlawing war. This was seized upon by Briand and signed by fifteen nations on 27 August 1928. But Hitler brushed this aside, saying that no one had the right to interfere in his rearmament programme or war preparations.

When Stresemann signed the Kellogg Pact in Germany's name he was convinced that Germany would never again start a war.

20. 'Action française' was a nationalist conservative movement which was critical of conditions in France. Many of its members later collaborated with the Hitler régime. As early as 1931 Hitler was already calculating on the advantages which his anti-semitism would bring him abroad. He was always expert at exploiting the anti-semitism and anti-marxism of conservative and chauvinist groups. He would select some socialist or Jewish politician and hold him up as responsible for the economic crisis, unemployment or what he called fallacious pacifist tendencies which ran counter to Germany's plans for rearmament. German politicians who planned some peaceful initiative in collaboration with foreign countries, were branded as traitors to their nation. Hitler believed that he could obtain England's approval of his international policy because, like the German bourgeoisie, England was afraid of bolshevism. In world politics England was cast in the same role as the German bourgeoisie at home.

21. Hitler claimed that he possessed information on Social Democrat collaboration with the Allies during the First World War. In fact, of course, he was trying to discredit the Social Democrats because he looked on them as the main pillar of the Weimar Republic. He used the Canadian Prime Minister's so-called revelations, published at the time, as proof of his stab-in-the-back theory. Hitler invariably blamed the Social Democrats for the isolated cases of espionage which took place during the war in order to present himself as the saviour of nationalist Germany.

22. On 20 June 1931 President Hoover proposed a moratorium for all international debts. Hitler showed great respect for Hoover and received him with the greatest ceremony after his seizure of power. He regarded Hoover and his friends as pro-German and

well-disposed towards him.

23. Although in the summer of 1931 Roosevelt was no more than the Governor of New York State, Hitler already regarded him as a politician who could be a danger to Germany, showing that he was well aware of Roosevelt's opinion of National-Socialism. 'Roosevelt and his political string-pullers' had frequently pointed out that National-Socialism would constitute a threat to Germany and Europe. Hitler regarded Roosevelt together with Churchill and Blum as coming politicians. Anyone who criticised his movement he placed upon his black list. The link between Hitler and certain circles in New York, London and Paris was his press officer Dr. Ernst (Putzi) Hanfstaengl; he had been at university with Roosevelt, was a friend of the Churchill family and an habitué of influential circles in Paris.

24. Hitler does not refer here to the encirclement of Germany, of which he made much in *Mein Kampf*. He says quite openly that there must be a showdown with Russia before America can intervene in Europe. As a preliminary he proposed to occupy by military force the states bordering on Germany to the east. He is in fact giving here a precise description of his subsequent annexationist eastern policy. On 3 February 1933, three days after his seizure of power, he visited General Hammerstein and told him that his first aim was accelerated rearmament and 'ruthless Germanisation' of the East. (Information from Frau Helga Rossow, the General's daughter.) On 28 February 1934, the anniversary of the Emergency Ordinance, Hitler assembled all Gruppenführer and Generals and told them solemnly that he had decided to build up a powerful modern army for the conquest of new *lebensraum*.

Hitler uses the term 'Inter-Europe' which had recently appeared in the press to describe the states lying between Germany and the Soviet Union from the Baltic to the Aegean. According to press reports this area was in chaos ethnically, economically and politically and the Germans were called upon to set it in order. Giselher Wirsing's book *Inter-Europe and the German Future* appeared in 1932.

25. Hitler expected great things from anti-semitic propaganda in England, France and other countries. In 1938 he contrived to obtain silent acquiescence from England and France for his eastern policy without having overt recourse to anti-semitism. At that time he had the strongest armed force in Europe and could strike at any moment. There was no lack of 'provocation' to justify such a step. The Munich agreement gave him a free hand for his moves against Czechoslovakia. The British acclaimed Chamberlain, thinking that they had avoided a world war. The result was seen six months later when Hitler occupied Czechoslovakia and turned it into a protectorate.

26. Hitler was determined to annex Austria as soon as he could and to complete his rearmament programme in five years. In 1936, three years after the seizure of power, he reoccupied the Rhineland, in 1938 he annexed Austria and in 1939 sparked off the war. He was determined to have Europe at Germany's mercy by the time he was fifty.

27. This shows that, even before he came to power, Hitler was toying with the idea of having other peoples as forced labourers; his policy was pure racialism with the Germans as colonisers for eastern Europe.

28. Once in power Hitler initiated a far-reaching anti-Comintern programme which culminated in the Three-Power Pact (Italy-Japan-Germany). From Europe Hungary, Slovakia, Rumania, Bulgaria and Yugoslavia joined this pact and from Asia Manchuria and Thailand. In the interim period Hitler signed a concordat with the Vatican and concluded a non-aggression pact between Germany and the Soviet Union.

29. Austria did not voluntarily join the Reich one year after the seizure of power. Instead there was an attempted *putsch* in Vienna in the course of which Dollfuss, the Chancellor, was murdered. In the same year King Alexander was murdered by fascist terrorists in France; Louis Barthou, the French Foreign Minister, was struck down at the same time.

30. This reference to the eternal values was a remarkably effective trick of demagogy on Hitler's part. He was incapable either of understanding them or of supporting their humanist aims.

31. This aspect of Hitler's ideology was one of the most dangerous because many people did not see through it. With his basic 'Law of the blood' Hitler destroyed or silenced the voice of reason or forced men of reason to emigrate. He was continually using the word 'Providence'. With semi-religious fervour Goebbels and Hess would proclaim that the Führer was the saviour and redeemer sent by God. So long as this germanic Messiah was alive no harm could come to the German people; he had been sent by Providence to expunge the shame of Germany. To give support and verisimilitude to this propagandist nonsense his associates engineered attacks to show that some supernatural force invariably protected him from the assaults of base and evil beings. Criminal police, the legal profession, judges and journalists were mobilised to add the weight of sensation to this 'evil deed propaganda'; the list included the Reichstag fire, the simulated attack near the Wagner memorial in Munich on 9 March 1933, the alleged attack on Göring in Unter den Linden on 21 March 1934, the fake attack on the Gleiwitz radio transmitter on 31 August 1939 and the Munich Bürgerbräukeller melodrama on 8 November 1939, synchronised with the kidnapping of two British Secret Service

officers in Venlo. From his cell Goerdeler was forced to announce both to the German people and the world at large that the failure of Stauffenberg's attack on the Führer was incontrovertible proof that he was under the protection of Providence and that this was the will of God.

32. Hitler laid down by law (see Note 11 to Introduction) that the 'Day of National Mourning' for the war dead and those who had fallen for the Party should be changed into 'Heroes Day'. On 25 February 1934 he celebrated the first 'Heroes Day' at Hindenburg's side in the Royal Box of the Opera House where he attended a Festival Performance. On 28 February, the anniversary of the day on which Hindenburg had signed the 'Ordinance for the Protection of People and State' giving Hitler the opportunity to rule anti-democratically, he assembled the Generals and Party leaders in Berlin and made a speech emphasising that he intended to form a new army and obtain for the German people the necessary *lebensraum*. The selection of this day too has a symbolic significance. Every year on 28 February the Junkers celebrated the birthday of Graf Schlieffen, the Prussian Chief of the General Staff (1833-1913), who had developed the theory of offensive warfare.

33. He did not do it in ten years but in twelve, by which time, in the name of 'the blood' he had committed more crimes than the previous thousand years of warfare could show.

34. In this interview Hitler revealed his fantastic, megalomaniac ideas on *lebensraum*. It is remarkable that, even before the war, he was working out plans for colonising both the East and the West. The best illustration of his criminal plans for the extermination of entire European peoples was Himmler's 'Overall Plan for the East'. After the occupation of France an SS staff was set up in Paris to draw the new ethnic 'nordic' line along the Loire. Once final victory had been won, accelerated germanisation was to be the fate of Northern France, Holland and Belgium.

35. Hitler's mention of Brittany and Burgundy did not imply that he proposed to form permanent states in these areas. The fragmentation of states and nations all over the continent suited his policy of political coercion and helped his resettlement and colonisation measures. As justification for his 'ruthless germanisation' he would quote the Goths' migrations and the discontent of the European minorities. The idea that the continent should bear the stamp of the Germans Hitler had culled from Houston Stewart Chamberlain's *Foundations of the Twentieth Century*. We are not dealing here with some anachronistic notion; moreover it is not true to say that Himmler and his staff were the only people to dream of the reorganisation of Europe. Hitler had his own ideas on the subject, as the talk with Breiting shows. Hitler hoped to win England and France over to his New Order by political

means. Should this not be possible, however, it would be done by war and partition. That does not mean that had London and Paris capitulated, the British and French Empires would have been saved. Capitulation would have been the first step leading to the installation of puppet Nazi governments in London and Paris. Sooner or later Hitler would have achieved his total transformation of Europe by means of brutal germanisation.

36. Dates and other comments in brackets are Breiting's additions. George Schönerer (1842-1921) was an Austrian pan-German and anti-Semite.

37. Hitler is referring to the Teutonic Knights who conquered and settled the Slav territories east of the Elbe. On 3 February 1933, only three days after becoming Chancellor, Hitler declared to an assembly of Army and Navy officers: 'The overall aim of our policy is the reconquest of political power.' Hitler talked of the capture of new markets but stressed that 'it would be far better to conquer new *lebensraum* in the East and subject it to ruthless germanisation'. (From notes by Otto von Heydebreck whose brother attended the conference.)

38. Hitler was quite right in saying that certain British circles were favourable to him and his policy. On the occasion of the 1936 Olympics, for instance, Hitler was presented with a photograph of Lloyd George with the inscription 'To Chancellor Hitler as a token of my admiration for his courage, determination and qualities as Führer'. Diana Mosley's and Unity Mitford's devotion to him are well known. Sir John Siddeley, the industrialist, looked upon Hitler as a friend. In 1932 Churchill and his entire family accompanied by Professor Lindemann journeyed to Munich to talk to Hitler. He refused to receive Churchill, however, not because he did not think that he carried weight in British politics, but because Churchill had criticised his anti-semitic policy. He left his visitors waiting in the Hotel Regina and refused to receive them. He had no wish to increase the respect in which Churchill was held.

39. At this period Herriot was one of the leaders of the Radical Socialist party in France, while Léon Blum was very little known in Germany. He had not yet become the leader of the Popular Front of 1936. Hitler, however, regarded him as a menace because he was of Jewish origin. The French Socialist party, particularly its German experts Salomon Grumbach and Georges Mandel, the subsequent Minister of the Interior, frequently drew the attention of the French public to the anti-semitic and fascist aspects of Hitler's policy. The fact that he referred to all these people shows how closely Hitler followed developments in France. During the Second World War Mandel was arrested and, on Hitler's orders, murdered by French collaborators because of his anti-Nazi views.

40. The Four-Power Pact 'for the preservation of peace' was signed in Rome on 16 July 1933 by Germany, Italy, England and France. Hitler's plans for the reconstitution of Europe naturally did not figure in it.

41. Alfred Graf von Schlieffen (1833-1913) was Chief of the Prussian General Staff from 1891-1906. In his study of the Battle of Cannae he developed the theory of total defeat of an enemy by rapid encirclement and annihilation. From these ideas the General Staff worked out a plan which, in a modified form, was used for the attack on France in 1914.

42. On 28 February 1933 Rosenberg, the editor of the *Völkischer Beobachter*, devoted his front page, not to the Reichstag fire, but to an article inspired by Hitler on the centenary of Schlieffen's birth. On 28 February 1934 Hitler celebrated the 101st anniversary of Schlieffen's birth before an assemblage of senior Reichswehr officers. In a secret speech he announced the formation of a modern army together with his decision to assure the German people adequate *lebensraum* in the East.

43. Hitler pretends to be convinced of the existence of some Jewish financial agency hostile to the aims of National-Socialism. In fact he was well aware that the Jews could approve neither his policy nor his claim to total power. He thought that, if he could eliminate the Jews as an intellectual and economic factor, his other opponents, Social Democrats, Christians and Liberals, would capitulate. He therefore deliberately dubbed all European politicians, including the communist party leaders, as 'Jewish lackeys' and 'puppets of world Jewry'. He repeated this deceptively simple slogan at intervals right up to the time of his death; it even appears in his testament of 30 April 1945, shortly before his suicide.

44. The intelligence service, formed by Hitler after the seizure of power, turned itself into the *Reichssicherheitshauptamt* (Central Security Department) in 1939. Section IV of this organisation, the Gestapo, ran a network of informers both at home and abroad, incarcerated people in prisons or concentration camps in 'protective custody', liquidated political and racial opponents and, with Section VI (Espionage abroad), organised fifth columns in other states. Kidnapping, beatings and murder were the methods employed by both sections. In addition to 7,000 senior officials the *Reichssicherheitshauptamt* had 70,000 other employees (see First Interview Note 10). Responsibility for the horrors of the past lies primarily upon the members of the *Reichssicherheitshauptamt*.

45. The fact that in one breath Hitler mentions the Young Plan, General Schleicher and the forthcoming Presidential elections is not a sign of illogicality. He both suspected and was *au fait* with Schleicher's efforts to reduce French pressure on Germany. Since

Hitler employed the crisis and the reparations burden as part of his propaganda, anyone who attempted to mitigate or remove them was in his eyes an enemy and a 'traitor'. In addition he knew that Schleicher was in favour of the re-election of Hindenburg and he himself was proposing to stand against him.

46. The result of the first ballot in the Presidential elections on 13 March 1932 was: Hitler 30·1 per cent, Hindenburg 49·6 per cent, Thälmann 13·2 per cent, Düsterberg (Stahlhelm) 6·8 per cent. Hindenburg was most disillusioned since he had to admit that many of the intelligentsia and the nationalist bourgeoisie had voted for Hitler.

47. In October 1931 there was a meeting in Harzburg between representatives of Hitler, Schacht and General von Seeckt representing the *Landbund* and the Stahlhelm, to find some method of 'national reconciliation'. When Hitler met Breiting he was preening himself about the results of the last elections in 1930 which had given him 107 seats in the Reichstag. In July 1932 his seats increased to 230. He did not capture 15 million votes, as he forecast to Breiting, but 13·7 million or 36·7 per cent. Nevertheless the National-Socialists were the strongest party and Hindenburg could not form a government with a majority in parliament. He was compelled to bolster up the government by using Article 48 of the Constitution, the Emergency Ordinance. Only a combination of Hitler and the German Nationals could now produce a parliamentary majority and so relieve Hindenburg of the accusation of being an authoritarian President.

48. Hitler's reference to von Papen, Hindenburg, Hugenberg and other conservative politicians was not fortuitous; the fact that eighteen months before the seizure of power he was looking to these men to help him shows his political acumen. He was intending to use anti-communism to demolish democracy and face them with the alternative: communism or National-Socialism. This in fact he did in January and February 1933. Hitler was very well informed about internal developments in other parties and knew the various personalities' political leanings. He also knew how important a role the Catholic Church could play in his seizure of power; in von Papen, a deputy in the Prussian Landtag and editor of the newspaper *Germania*, he saw the man who could put him in touch with the Herrenklub and so with Hindenburg and the Vatican. In January 1933 it was von Papen who conducted the negotiations with Hindenburg and became Hitler's Vice-Chancellor. In the spring of that year he negotiated the Concordat with the Vatican which was signed on 22 July. The precision with which Hitler adhered to his 'schedule' is remarkable.

49. The book concerned was *Der Mythus des 20 Jahrhunderts* (Myth of the Twentieth Century), published in 1930. It is interesting

to note that Hitler attributes no political importance to Rosenberg, his ideological expert, although he was editor of the *Völkischer Beobachter*. Hitler certainly did not express this opinion so that Breiting could pass it on; he was already convinced that sooner or later he would need the right wing of the Centre. He hoped to be able to detach Brüning from the left wing and so use the Centre for his 'national reawakening'. At this point von Papen had no inkling of the role in which Hitler had cast him. Hitler, however, knew that like Hugenberg and many of the Generals, von Papen was dreaming of a change in the constitution or of a monarchy – and Hitler was not going to stop them dreaming. For him the only important point was that he should be able to include them in his anti-communist front. Brüning and Papen were not among those who made the pilgrimage to Harzburg for the nationalist meeting in the autumn of 1931. In his recent book (*Vom Scheitern einer Demokratie*) von Papen considers that Brüning missed an opportunity by failing to join the Harzburg Front. How naïve! By 1931 Hitler was already head and shoulders above his opponents and future allies as a tactician and politician. How accurate his calculations were is proved by the fact that as early as 1931 he was reckoning upon a capitulation by the Centre and visualising a Concordat with the Vatican. Hitler's statements to Breiting show that he was no improviser but a cold-blooded calculator who knew how to use the right language in private discussions. The seizure of power was no accident resulting from Hindenburg's appointment of von Papen; it happened because Hitler had decided on the phases of his assault by 1931 or even earlier. In thinking that they could relegate Hitler to the rear rank Hitler's coalition partners merely gave proof of their political naïveté. As things turned out, whether from opportunism or patriotism, they did their best to destroy the Weimar Republic and turn Hitler into the Dictator of the Third Reich. Breiting's interviews prove that the 'Führer' had given mature consideration to his every move before and after the seizure of power. They also show that there were many who knew what Hitler's aims were, approved of them and assisted him. He succeeded not because people found his gaze seducing and bewitching but because he clung to his devilish purposes with iron determination.

50. The 'resettlement programme' referred to by Hitler would have driven millions upon millions from their homes, both opponents and supporters, both 'Aryans' and 'non-Aryans'. To ensure a germanic preponderance 'impure elements' were to be destroyed in millions. Colossal concentration camps, castration and sterilisation centres, and gas chambers with far greater 'output' than Auschwitz were planned. The euthanasia experts, the *Einsatzgruppen*, the static or mobile gas chambers were only the craftsmen precursors of the planned indus-

trialised conveyor-belt murder machine.

51. Captain Ernst Röhm fled abroad after the failure of the 1923 *putsch* and the resulting ban on paramilitary formations. As a friend and confidant of Hitler he was recalled in 1930 to be Chief of Staff of the SA. Even Himmler as Reichsführer-SS was subordinate to him. In 1934 Hitler engineered a *coup* against him and General von Schleicher, accusing them of preparing a *putsch* against him. To bring Göring to the post, a simulated attack against him was arranged for 21 March 1934. A painter named Erwin Schulze, a member of the opposition, was accused of having thrown a hand grenade from the top floor window of a house on Unter den Linden. The grenade landed on the car of David Oliver, a Jewish financier from Vienna. The criminal police 'treated' Schulze and extracted a 'confession' that he was acting as a lone wolf, after having first tried to persuade him to admit that he had obtained the hand grenade from the Reichswehr. After the trial Hindenburg received a secret report to the effect that, whatever the court may have said, Schulze could only have obtained his grenade from the Reichswehr; he had been a Reichswehr cadet trained in grenade throwing. His former fellow-cadets and members of his family were cited as witnesses. For the sake of the Reichswehr's reputation both at home and abroad, however, people did not wish to implicate it. Meanwhile the Gestapo pursued their investigations. On 30 June 1934 came the showdown with the opposition both in the Party and the Reichswehr; Schleicher and his wife were murdered in Berlin on 30 June and Röhm in Munich-Stadelheim on 1 July. Even today this criminal proceeding is still presented by ex-dignitaries of the Third Reich and Himmler's SA informers as if Hitler had been the victim of false information. Some are even prepared to maintain that there was real evidence of a *putsch* against Hitler and that the Führer's measures were fully justified.

52. Sheer envy was the reason for Hitler's opposition to America's Great Power policy, that of Russia in the future and the French and British colonial empires. He used them merely to justify his far more grandiose plans. He was not interested in the liberation of 'oppressed' races or in raising the standard of living of the German people. There was no social doctrine in his movement. The workers were subjected to political discipline simply in order that they might forge weapons for the conquest both of the East and the West. The sources of raw materials which Hitler demanded were intended to serve, not to raise the standard of life of his people, but his plans for world conquest. The autobahns, constructed in such haste, were part of the preparations for motorised warfare. Five years after the seizure of power Hitler had the greatest military force in the world. War could begin.

NOTES AND COMMENTS

53. Otto Braun was Minister-President of Prussia, Karl Severing Minister of the Interior and Albert Grzesinski Police President of Berlin.

54. Hitler is making play here with the words of a Bavarian deputy who shouted out in the Reichstag: 'Better to die a Bavarian than go to the dogs as a Prussian.'

55. Though tactically Hitler was an improviser, he always remained faithful to his strategy. At his first cabinet meeting on 30 January 1933 he opposed the suppression of the communist party. Hugenberg, his coalition partner, would have preferred to ban the communist party than call new elections, but Hitler insisted on elections since they would open for him the way to total power. He had no wish to play the policeman on behalf of the bourgeoisie and he used the pretext of the threat of a general strike. With the Reichswehr behind him he wished to inflict an electoral defeat on the communists. Hugenberg was forced to give way and accept fresh elections. Once they were over, the communist party was banned.

56. These are no idle words from Hitler. Historic names had both a symbolic and practical significance for him. He made his last election speech (on 4 March 1933) in Königsberg. On 21 March, at a ceremony in Potsdam, Hindenburg confirmed him in his position as Chancellor.

57. The 'Gleichschaltung' of all the *Länder* took place on 30 January 1934, exactly a year after the seizure of power, when all Germany was united under a centralised administration .

58. Goebbels established the Berlin Party newspaper *Angriff*.

59. The Reichswehr Ministry administered 21 infantry regiments, 18 cavalry regiments, 7 artillery regiments, some engineer battalions, transport detachments and signals and naval units.

60. This shows that, even two years before coming to power, Hitler had a clear picture of the concentration camps in his mind. The transformation of the criminal police into an instrument of political repression Hitler later entrusted to Heinrich Müller, a Bavarian police official, later promoted Head of the Gestapo. Müller was probably one of those police officers with whom Hitler was in touch before the seizure of power.

61. Hitler's figures are wrong.

62. Despite his aversion to the Black Army, for a whole year after coming to power Hitler allowed the paramilitary formations to be armed and trained by Reichswehr headquarters.

63. On 1 April 1931 ex-Captain Stennes, commander of the Berlin SA, refused to obey Hitler's orders. The SA rebellion was put down by the Berlin SS under Kurt Daluege.

64. After the suppression of the Stennes *putsch* Hitler wrote Daluege a letter in which he coined the famous phrase: 'Loyalty

is thine honour,' later the motto of the SS.

65. The interview shows that Hitler was determined to organise a powerful Secret Service. That summer he commissioned Himmler, the Reichsführer-SS, to reorganise the security service. A few months after this interview Reinhard Heydrich, an ex-Naval Lieutenant, took over.

66. On every conceivable occasion Hitler repeated stereotyped phrases which he had learnt by heart. Both these ideas and the exact words are to be found in his reply to the Reichstag debate on the Enabling Law on 23 March 1933, when he accused the Social Democrats of treason and maintained that they were responsible for Germany's defeat in the First World War (the stab-in-the-back theory).

67. As a result of Hitler's attitude many of the best and most competent Jewish brains went abroad after the seizure of power. They created no unrest among his enemies; in fact they helped to produce the scientific and technical instruments which smashed the Nazi war machine.

68. After his seizure of power Hitler expanded his political and paramilitary formations to do just this – Hitler Youth, SA, SS, NSKK (National Socialist Motor Corps), Labour Service etc.

69. Not until the end of 1931 did Breiting learn that Heydrich's Leipzig contact had reported that he was exerting an anti-Nazi influence among the German Nationalists. When Hitler came to power the *Leipziger Neueste Nachrichten* was an ardent supporter of the coalition. Breiting was not labelled as a 'Jewish lackey' or persecuted until early 1934. Frank, Hess and Goerdeler prevented him being arrested. On paper he remained editor of the paper so that his contacts could be used.

70. From the note on which the discussion ended it is clear that Hitler regarded Breiting's second visit as a means of approach to the German Nationals. This is also supported by the fact that Hitler was very well informed on developments in Saxony and in high level conservative circles there. On 20 August 1931 Wilhelm Bünger, an ex-Minister-President of Saxony and a personal friend of Breiting, was appointed President of the Reich Court. Two years later, at Hitler's behest, he conducted the notorious Reichstag Fire Trial which lasted from 21 September to 23 December 1933.

71. When Hitler decided to send his new Wehrmacht into Austria, he thought the time had come to rid himself of his Army opponents and assume control of the Wehrmacht himself. He commissioned Heydrich to produce some well thought out plot to deal with Field Marshal Blomberg and Colonel-General Fritsch. Much still remains to be revealed about these machinations. Göring who was President of the Court of Honour on Fritsch, was clearly unable to forget Heydrich's intrigues of 1933 and 1934 during the

struggle for control of the Gestapo and, when it became obvious that Fritsch had fallen victim to Himmler's and Heydrich's machinations, Hitler was forced by pressure from various officers to appoint Fritsch Colonel-in-Chief of No. 12 Artillery Regiment for the invasion of Poland. Rehabilitation of Fritsch, however, did not suit Hitler and his SS myrmidons at all and Colonel-General Fritsch had to die for his Führer in front of Warsaw on 22 August 1939. There was talk of suicide. Hitler ordered a State funeral which, however, he did not attend. Thenceforth any senior officer was afraid that he might be 'honoured' with a State funeral. In all probability Fritsch was liquidated like Rommel. Hitler wanted no generals of the old school who insisted on their conception of military administration in occupied territory. He wanted officers like General Eduard Wagner, the later Quarter-Master General, who, by his agreement with Heydrich, handed the civil population over to the mercies of the SS thugs. Fritsch would never have been invited into Himmler's special train, but Wagner visited it and bragged about the visit in his diary. The bullets which killed Schleicher and Bredow and Fritsch's 'hero's death' before Warsaw were warning shots for Wagner and other opportunists. Wagner died in mysterious circumstances after 20 July 1944. Kaltenbrunner's report says that he committed suicide, but the matter has never been fully cleared up. Many officers liquidated by Hitler are said to have 'chosen death'.

Epilogue

1. After only three days as Chancellor, Brüning circulated to his cabinet colleagues a constitutional memorandum putting forward the view that the agreement of Parliament was not necessary for the appointment or dismissal of a Minister of the Reich; a cabinet could govern based on Article 48 (the emergency article) and the confidence of the Reich President. This was completely at variance with Article 54 of the constitution under which the Chancellor and Ministers must have the confidence of the Reichstag. Hitler did not forget this memorandum nor the procedure which developed therefrom and was carried on by von Papen and Schleicher. They had blazed for him the 'legal road to power' without Reichstag agreement. He did not intend to use Article 48 to protect the Republic, however, but to destroy it.

2. In this Stresemann followed the example of Walther Rathenau who, on 16 April 1922, signed the Treaty of Rapallo re-establishing diplomatic relations between Germany and Russia.

3. Karl-Dietrich Bracher has made a penetrating analysis of the electoral results. Though he did so without knowledge of the

Hitler-Breiting conversations, he comes to the conclusion that, despite his adroit propaganda Hitler did not succeed in changing the structural basis of the electorate and that he would never have come to power by democratic methods (*Die Auflösung der Weimarer Republik*, Villingen 1960).

4. As early as May 1918 the 'German Workers Party in Austria' changed its name to 'German National-Socialist Workers Party'. In January 1919 Drexler and Harrer, the founders of a similar party in Munich, decided to include 'National-Socialist' in the title of their movement. As we know, Hitler joined this group and soon took over the leadership.

5. The National-Socialist Reich was to be the 'Third' or 'Greater German' Reich. The expression was based, not so much on history – Holy Roman Empire from 962 to 1806, Hohenzollern Empire from 1871 to 1918 – as on the 'Third' or 'eternal' Reich of the mediaeval sagas. The notion was popularised in a book entitled *Das Dritte Reich* by Arthur Moeller van den Bruck, a member of the Young Conservatives, written in praise of Prussianism. The phrase occurs in the Nazi battle song 'Many fell in Munich', part of the refrain being 'There are still thousands of fighters for the Third Reich, the Greater German Reich'.

6. Hitler said to Breiting: 'Whatever guarantees the vital interests of the nation is legal.' We shall be reverting later to his 'juridical concept'.

7. The Reichswehr Generals both admired and feared the way in which Hitler had built up his secret service and paramilitary formations. Conservative politicians such as Hugenberg were much impressed by the capacity for repartee shown by Hitler during his debate with Wels, the socialist leader, on the Enabling Law on 23 March 1933.

8. The figures are taken from Hitler's 1932 New Year's Message (*Völkischer Beobachter* 1/2 January 1932). They show that almost 50 per cent of the Party membership belonged to the paramilitary formations. Their numbers were not far short of the million which Hitler considered necessary to face the bourgeoisie with the 'bolshevism or National-Socialism' alternative.

9. The fact that Hitler attached more importance to a take-over of the police than to the formation of a cabinet is proved by a conversation which took place on 29 January 1933 between him, von Papen and Göring. Von Papen records it as follows: 'As far as Prussia was concerned both Hitler and Göring pointed out that the police had been in socialist hands for more than five years and that they must be purged before they could be of value for use against communist terrorism' (*Vom Scheitern einer Demokratie*, p. 381).

10. Discussion of the various factions among the Generals

resulting from the internal political situation is outside the scope of this book. It is merely worth recording that, through his secret service, Hitler succeeded in dividing the officer corps and partially winning it over. Pro-Hitler officers played a decisive role in the dismissal of Schleicher from the Chancellorship and influenced Hindenburg to appoint Hitler. By the end of 1932 Hitler had his 'agents' everywhere and they prevented Schleicher being appointed Reichswehr Minister in the coalition cabinet, saying that he was preparing a *putsch* and wished to have Hindenburg interned.

Giselher Wirsing, the journalist, believes that these reports were not fabricated and that von Schleicher and von Hammerstein really did intend to do something against Hitler, perhaps even arrest him (see *Christ und Welt*, 25 January 1963). Kunrat von Hammerstein, the General's son, however disputes the fact that there was ever any such intention.

11. Hitler told Breiting also that the Germans alone had great technical achievements to their credit. It is superfluous to point out that science was making great progress in every country and that, as Joliot-Curie once put it, 'research requires no visa'. In fact, by their energy and knowledge, the men expelled from Germany contributed much to the defence of the free world. When I met Wernher von Braun at a convention in 1958 he said to me: 'Scientific advance is merely a question of the money allocated to the scientists.'

12. Hitler's electoral speeches in the first half of 1932 in Domarus *Hitler – Reden und Proklamationen*, Süddeutscher Verlag, Munich 1965.

13. Reichswehr officers appeared with troops and arrested Otto Braun, the Minister-President, Karl Severing, the Minister of the Interior, Albert Grzesinski, the Police President of Berlin and Bernhard Weiss, the Vice-President. The commander of the Berlin *Schutzpolizei* (Regular police) and several senior Prussian officials were dismissed.

14. If Hitler had insisted on arguing his right to the Chancellorship, the audience would never have taken place. The current rumour was that Hindenburg had said that the 'Bohemian corporal' would never cross the threshold of his residence in the Wilhelmstrasse as long as he lived. The audience gave the lie to this rumour. Hitler had crossed the Rubicon.

15. This interview, like that between Hitler and Breiting, had been arranged by Otto Dietrich, the Nazi Party press chief. It shows that Hitler and his associates were expert at differentiating between ideas suitable for the masses and those destined for prominent members of the intelligentsia and bourgeoisie.

16. This text was found among Breiting's papers. It tallies with notes made by other shorthand writers present. Unfortunately

Oberfohren's speech has been disregarded by many historians.

17. Von Papen, *Vom Scheitern einer Demokratie*, p. 385.

18. At this point the coalition consisted of 196 National-Socialist deputies and 52 German Nationals out of a total of 584 in the Reichstag. The two parties had captured only 14·8 million votes out of a total electorate of 44·3 million. Brüning, von Papen and Schleicher having failed with Article 48 of the constitution, no internal or external threat justified Hindenburg appointing Hitler Chancellor. The other parties, which constituted the majority, were obviously discredited. The German Nationals had found their partner at last. Oberfohren had to bow to the inevitable.

19. In his *Memoirs* von Papen refers to the Reichstag fire as one of the arguments used by Hitler to extract the Emergency Ordinance from Hindenburg. He says that according to Rudolf Diels, the Head of the Gestapo, and Helmut Heisig of the Criminal Police, the Nazis were not responsible for the fire. In his later book Hitler's ex-Vice-Chancellor has not the face to mention these 'witnesses'.

20. The speech was made on 10 October 1932 to the members of the 'Volksdienst' recruiting centre in Berlin, while von Papen was still Chancellor.

21. *Mein Kampf* (Murphy's translation) p. 205.

22. Compiled from Cuno Horkenbach's *Das Deutsche Reich von 1918 bis heute*, Berlin 1933.

23. The Berlin vote was a particular disappointment to Hitler. (He had told Breiting that Berlin was a 'muckheap'.) Despite the Nazi terror, at the 5 March 1933 elections the Social Democrats and communists gained 53 per cent of the votes in Berlin against the Nazi 31 per cent. In all 69 per cent of Berliners voted against the Nazis. Even with his allies, the German Nationals, Hitler had a bare 40 per cent.

24. It was well known abroad that Oberfohren was an anti-Nazi and knew a great deal about the background to the Reichstag fire. On 26/27 April 1933 the *Manchester Guardian* published an 'Oberfohren Memorandum' on the subject but this was merely an anti-Hitler inflammatory pamphlet.

25. Before his death his party forced Oberfohren, as floor leader, to sign the motion for the Enabling Law and vote for the change in the constitution. Whether from fear or opportunism, many others also conformed.

26. After Klausener's murder Hitler issued a communiqué stating that he had shot himself to avoid arrest. After 1945 Gildisch, the SS man detailed by Heydrich as the murderer, stated that on orders from above he had shot Klausener and pressed a pistol into his hand to simulate suicide.

27. According to Breiting's notes, on 5 May 1933 Goebbels

despatched Karl Hanke of his staff to Kiel to settle the matter. On 10 May 1933 Hugenberg said to Breiting: 'The murder of Ober-fohren was intended to silence a brave man and frighten the rest to death.'

28. *Mein Kampf* (Murphy's translation) p. 204.

29. Secret letter of 1934 from Diels to Göring – in secret Prussian State Archives, Berlin.

30. Original letter of 1933 (in my possession) from Willi Thamm, the 'King of the Berlin Thugs' to one of Gestapo Müller's staff.

31. It is not the purpose of this epilogue, nor is it necessary here, to produce proof of how Hitler trapped van der Lubbe nor of his horrible treatment in prison before his execution; we are merely concerned with National-Socialist ideology and their *coup d'état* technique. I have devoted a special study to the whole question of the Reichstag fire; based on criminological and technological research this proves conclusively that a handful of SS men under Daluege and Heydrich carried out Hitler's orders and set the building on fire. The blame for this crime cannot therefore be attributed to the SA, as is generally assumed and erroneously reported abroad. Ideologically the SA was too untrustworthy for Hitler to have entrusted them with a secret of this magnitude.

32. *Reichsgesetzblatt* (Official Gazette) 1934, p. 529.

33. Hans Günther, a public prosecutor, in his monograph *Bewältigung der Vergangenheit*, Berlin, April 1967.

34. In the September/October 1941 issue of *Kriminalistik*, a periodical edited by Heydrich, SS-Obersturmbannführer (Lieu-tenant-Colonel) and Criminal Police Director Walter Zirpins wrote an article headed 'The Lodz ghetto from the Criminal Police view-point'. In it he said that he found this 'new field of activity fascinat-ing, interesting from many angles and professionally gratifying, in other words satisfying'. Zirpins and his ilk are now the main witnesses to the legend that Hitler did not set the Reichstag on fire and, moreover, that he had no need to do so since the entire German people was already behind him. History does not relate that the entire German people would have found work in the Lodz ghetto as fascinating as did Zirpins.

35. Judgement of 21 April 1967 on the plea by the Public Prosecutor for annulment of the death sentence pronounced by the Reich Court in Leipzig on 23 December 1933. It is legitimate to wonder whether the primary object of the Berlin judges in awarding van der Lubbe eight years imprisonment was not to impress upon the world the German people's 'lack of instinct' and their collective responsibility for the court's decision. This would be equivalent to condemning all those who question whether Hitler came to power legally and in accordance with the will of the people.

In his book *Hitlers unbeachtete Maximen* [Hitler's unconsidered maxims] published in 1968, Professor Karl Lange has given a masterly description of Hitler's capacity to conceal his true character and his plans behind a screen of professions of legality and assurances of peace; he even misled people by saying that his book *Mein Kampf* was a thing of the past. Yet of the millions of copies of the 'Nazi bible' sold or given away, only some 10 per cent were read. It was understood only by a few of his enemies and by the Nazi 'élite'. Once Goebbels had laid hands on the propaganda media and Himmler on the police machine, it was not only useless but dangerous to preach to the public at large any idea of resistance. The Nazi hydra could only be killed by the war which it had itself instigated.

Hitler regarded General Erich Ludendorff (1865-1937), the ex-Quarter-Master-General of World War I, as the theorist of total war and he told Breiting that he had learnt from Ludendorff many of the political and strategic ideas set out in *Mein Kampf*; yet Ludendorff eventually rejected him. In 1922 Ludendorff was leader of the German Popular Freedom Party and he took part in the Nazi *putsch* in Munich in November 1923. Like many other conservatives, he hoped to be able to use the Hitler movement for his own ends; he thought that through the Nazi movement he could gain control of the army and, as head of the German armed forces, in practice rule the country; he would then assault the Versailles Treaty in his own way. He soon realised, however, that Hitler regarded himself not only as a politician but as a strategist and so, in 1928, he split with Hitler and declared open political warfare on him; he even wrote articles on 'war psychosis and genocide'. On 15 October 1927 Stephan Grossmann wrote in *Tagebuch*, then a widely read periodical: 'If he (Ludendorff) had wished, how easy it would have been for him, the warlord of the First World War, to play a decisive role in the Weimar Republic – or at least among the right-wing parties ... But Ludendorff did not want to.' It is not generally known that Ludendorff warned both Hindenburg and the Generals against the National-Socialists. It is outside the scope of this book to cite all the treatises and articles which Ludendorff wrote pointing out that Hitler would lead Germany to catastrophe. This did not prevent Hitler, the demagogue, however, from going to Ludendorff's deathbed to demonstrate to the world that there were no differences between them. Not all officers who were against Versailles can be labelled as war-mongers and supporters of the policy of conquest. Still less can an entire people be held responsible for what happened in 1933 through the manipulation an élite. If the vast majority of the people had been listened to, there would have been no wars of conquest, no Sachsenhausen, no Buchenwald, no Dachau, no Mauthausen, no Auschwitz.

SOURCES

Information orally or in writing from:

Richard Breiting's papers

Frau Emmy Breiting

Otto von Heydebreck, correspondent of the *Basler Nachrichten*

Shorthand record of a speech by Ernst Oberfohren to the Deutsche Gesellschaft in November 1932

Paul Löbe, President of the Reichstag 1920-1932

Franz von Papen, Reich Chancellor 1932, Vice-Chancellor under Hitler 1933-4

André François-Poncet, French Ambassador, Berlin

Dr. Otto Strasser, author, Munich

Blagoj Popoff, Minister Plenipotentiary Sofia, one of the accused in the Reichstag Fire Trial

Frau Doris Hertwig-Bünger, widow of Dr. Wilhelm Bünger, President of the Reich Court

Bishop Erich Klausener, Berlin

Pastor Heinrich Grüber, Berlin

Professor Emil Dovifat, Berlin

Milivoj Pandurovic, Consul-General (retd.) Belgrade

Professor Vaso Bogdanov, member of the Jugoslav Academy of Science, Zagreb

Professor Golo Mann, Zurich

Josef Kojetski, Czech journalist murdered in a concentration camp

Dr. Ernst Hanfstaengl, publicist, Munich

Edmond Forschbach, civil servant, Bonn

Professor Jens Jessen, executed after 20 July 1944

Professor Carlo Schmid, Federal Minister, Bonn

Dr. Friedrich Zipfel, Meinecke Institute, Berlin

Arno Scholz, editor of the *Telegraf*, Berlin

Professor Tadeusz Cieslak, Warsaw

Ludwig Krieger, senior civil servant, head of the Reichstag stenographic bureau and shorthand writer in the Führer's headquarters

Erwin Schulze, painter, unjustly sentenced to ten years imprisonment for a supposed attack on Göring on 21 March 1934

UNMASKED

Frau Annedore Leber, Berlin
Theo Hespers, leader of Catholic Youth in the Rhineland, murdered in 1943
Dr. Robert M. W. Kempner, Lansdowne, USA
Dr. Hans-Bernd Gisevius, ex-civil servant, St. Légier
Professor Didrich Arup Seip, Rector of Oslo University
Piet Jongeling, Netherlands Deputy
Gottfried Reinhold Treviranus, Minister of the Reich 1930-1932
Libraries, archives and document centres in Germany, Austria and France

BIBLIOGRAPHY

Adolph, Walter: *Erich Klausener*, Morus Verlag, Berlin 1955

Baschwitz, Kurt: *Der Massenwahn*, C. H. Beck, Munich 1932

Bayle, F.: *Psychologie et Ethique du National-Socialisme*, Presse Universitaire, Paris 1953

Bismarck, Otto von: *Gedanken und Erinnerungen*, Cotta, Stuttgart and Berlin 1913

Bennecke, Heinrich: *Hitler und die SA*, Olzog Verlag, Munich and Vienna 1962

Bennecke, Heinrich: *Die Reichswehr und der 'Röhm-Putsch'*, Olzog Verlag, Munich and Vienna 1964

Berndt, Alfred Ingemar: *Meilensteine des Dritten Reiches*, Franz Eher, Munich 1938

Boelcke, Willi A.: *Deutschlands Rüstung im Zweiten Weltkrieg*, Philips, Frankfurt 1969

Bor, Peter: *Gespräche mit Halder*, Limes Verlag, Wiesbaden 1950

Bracher, Karl-Dietrich: *Die Auflösung der Weimarer Republik*, Ring-Verlag, Stuttgart and Düsseldorf 1955

Bracher, Karl-Dietrich: *Stufen totalitärer Gleichschaltung*, Vierteljahreshefte für Zeitgeschichte, Stuttgart, No. 1 of 1956

Bracher, Karl-Dietrich: *Die Deutsche Diktatur*, Kiepenheuer and Witsch, Cologne 1969

Bracher, Karl-Dietrich/Sauer, Wolfgang and Schulz, Gerhard: *Die nationalsozialistische Machtergreifung*, Westdeutsche Verlag, Cologne and Opladen 1962

Braun, Otto: *Von Weimar bis Hitler*, Europa Verlag, Hamburg 1949

Bross, Werner: *Gespräche mit Göring*, Wolff Verlag, Flensburg and Hamburg 1950

180

BIBLIOGRAPHY

Broszat, Martin: 'The Concentration Camps', translated Marian Jackson, in *Anatomy of the SS State*, Collins, London 1968

Buchheim, Hans: 'The SS – Instrument of Domination', translated Richard Barry, in *Anatomy of the SS State*, Collins, London 1968

Bullock, Alan: *Hitler, a Study in Tyranny*, Revised Edition, Penguin Books, Harmondsworth 1962

Calic Edouard: *Himmler et son Empire*, Série Témoins de notre Temps, Paris 1966

Calic, Edouard: *Le Reichstag brûle*, Opéra Mundi, Paris 1969

Caro, Kurt and Oehme, Walter: *Schleicher's Aufstieg*, Rowohlt, Berlin 1933.

Churchill, Winston S.: *The Second World War*, Cassell and Co., London 1952

Clausewitz, Carl von: *Hinterlassene Werke über Kriege und Kriegsführung*, Ferdinand Dümmlers Verlagsbuchhandlung, Berlin 1857

Crankshaw, Edward: *The Gestapo*, Putnam, London 1956

Czech-Jochberg, E.: *Hitler, eine deutsche Bewegung*, Gerhard Stalling Verlag, Oldenburg 1930

Deborin, G. A.: *Der zweite Weltkrieg*, Berlin 1960

Delarue, Jacques: *The History of the Gestapo,* translated Mervyn Savill, Macdonald, London 1964

Delmer, Sefton: *Autobiography*, Secker and Warburg, London 1961-2

Deutsch, Harold C.: *Verschwörung gegen den Krieg*, Beck, Munich 1969

Diels, Rudolf: *Lucifer ante Portas*, Deutsche Verlagsanstalt, Stuttgart 1950

Dimitroff, Georgi: *Le procès de Leipzig*, Sofia 1964

Domarus, Max: *Hitler – Reden und Proklamationen*, Süddeutscher Verlag, Munich 1965

Dovifat, Emil: *Allgemeine Publizistik I*, Berlin 1968

Dovifat, Emil: *Praktische Publizistik*, Berlin 1968

Dubost, Charles: *Le Procès de Nuremberg*, Service Crimes de Guerre, Paris 1947

Duesterberg, Theodor: *Der Stahlhelm und Hitler*, Wolfenbüttler Verlag, Wolfenbüttel 1949

Eschenburg, Theodor: *Staat und Gesellschaft in Deutschland*, Schwab, Stuttgart 1956

Eschenburg, Theodor: *Die Rolle der Persönlichkeit in der Weimarer Republik, Vierteljahreshefte für Zeitgeschichte*, Stuttgart 1961

Faure, Edgar: *La Condition Humaine sous la Domination Nazie*, Office française d'édition, Paris 1946

UNMASKED

François-Poncet, André: *The Fateful Years*, translated Jacques Le Clercq, Victor Gollancz, London 1948

Fritsch, Theodor: *Die Zionistische Protokolle*, Hammerverlag, Leipzig 1924

de Gaulle, Charles: *Memoirs – Call to Honour*, Collins, London 1955; *Unity*, Weidenfeld & Nicolson, London 1959

Gilbert, G. M.: *Nuremberg Diary*, New American Library, New York 1947

Gisevius, H.-B.: *Adolf Hitler*, Rütten and Loening, Munich 1963

Goebbels, Joseph: *Vom Kaiserhof zur Reichskanzlei*, Franz Eher, Munich 1934

Goebbels, Joseph: *Wetterleuchten*, Franz Eher, Munich 1943

Görlitz, Walter: *The German General Staff*, Hollis and Carter, London 1953

Görlitz, Walter: *Der Zweite Weltkrieg*, Steingruben Verlag, Stuttgart, 1951-2

Görlitz, Walter and Quint, Herbert A.: *Adolf Hitler*, Steingruben Verlag, Stuttgart 1952

Grüber, Heinrich: *Erinnerungen aus sieben Jahrzehnten*, Kiepenheuer & Witsch, Cologne 1968

Günther, Hans: *Bewältigung der Vergangenheit*, lecture in Berlin, April 1967

Haffner, Sebastian, *Der grosse Verrat*, Die Stern 1968

Hagen, Walter: *J'étais le Faussaire de Hitler*, Duca, Paris 1956

Halder, Franz: *Hitler als Feldherr*, Dom Verlag, Munich 1949

Hammerstein, Kunrat Freiherr von: *Schleicher, Hammerstein und die Machtübernahme*, Frankfurter Hefte 1/56-3/56, Frankfurt 1956

Hanfstaengl, Ernst: *Hitler – The Missing Years*, Eyre & Spottiswoode, London 1957

Heer, Friedrich: *Der Glaube des Adolf Hitler*, Bechtle Verlag, Munich 1968

Heiber, Helmut: *Adolf Hitler*, Colloquium Verlag, Berlin 1960

Heiden, Konrad: *Hitler*, Europa Verlag, Zurich 1936

Heinrich, Wolfgang: *Meister der Kriminalistik*, Universitäts Verlag, Berlin 1955

Hess, Rudolf: *Reden*, Franz Eher, Munich 1937

Hillgruber, Andreas: *Hitlers Strategie*, Bernard & Graefe, Frankfurt 1965

Hitler, Adolf: *Mein Kampf*, translated J. Murphy, Hurst & Blackett, London 1939

Hitler, Adolf: *Reden und Proklamationen*, edited by Max Domarus, Süddeutscher Verlag, Munich 1965

182

BIBLIOGRAPHY

Hofer, Walther: *Der Nationalsozialismus*, Fischer Bücherei, Frankfurt 1957

Hofer, Walther: *Die Entfesselung des Zweiten Weltkrieges*, Fischer Bücherei, Frankfurt 1960

Horkenbach, Bruno: *Das Deutsche Reich von 1918 bis heute, Handbuch des Reichs- und Staatsbehörden*, Berlin 1933

Hull, Cordell: *Memoirs*, Hodder & Stoughton, London 1948

Jacobsen, Hans-Adolf: *Der Zweite Weltkrieg in Chronik und Dokumenten*, Wehr und Wissen Verlagsgesellschaft, Darmstadt 1959

Jacobsen, Hans-Adolf: 'The Kommissar-befehl and Mass Executions of Soviet Russian Prisoners of War', translated Dorothy Long, in *Anatomy of the SS State*, Collins, London 1968

Kempner, Robert M. W.: *SS im Kreuzverhör*, Rütten & Loening, Munich 1964

Kempner, Robert M. W.: *Edith Stein und Anne Frank*, Freiburg 1968

Kogon, Eugen: *The Theory and Practice of Hell*, translated Heinz Norden, Secker & Warburg, London 1950

Kordt, Erich: *Nicht aus den Akten*, Union Deutsche Verlagsgesellschaft, Stuttgart 1950

Krausnick, Helmut: 'The Persecution of the Jews', translated Dorothy Long, in *Anatomy of the SS State*, Collins, London 1968

Lange, Karl: *Hitlers unbeachtete Maximen*, Kohlhammer, Stuttgart 1968

Last, Jef: *Kruisgang der Jeugd*, Rotterdam 1939

Last, Jef: *Rinus van der Lubbe*, Dinxperlo 1967

Ludendorff, Erich: *Der totale Krieg*, Ludendorffs Verlag, Munich 1936

Ludendorff, Mathilde: *Erich Ludendorff*, Ludendorffs Verlag, Munich 1940

Löbe, Paul: *Erinnerungen eines Reichstagspräsidenten*, Arani Verlag, Berlin 1949

Löbe, Paul: *Der Weg war lang*, Arani Verlag, Berlin 1954

Lüdecke, Karl: *I knew Hitler*, Jarrolds, London 1938

Malanowski, Wolfgang: *November Revolution*, E. Klett, Berlin 1969

Malraux, André: *Antimemoirs*, translated Terence Kilmartin, Hamish Hamilton, London 1968

Manstein, Erich von: *Lost Victories*, translated A. G. Powell, Methuen, London 1958

Manvell, Roger and Fraenkel, Heinrich: *Doctor Goebbels*, New

English Library, London 1968

Manvell, Roger and Fraenkel, Heinrich: *The Incomparable Crime*, Wm. Heinemann, London 1967

Maser, Werner: *Hitler's 'Mein Kampf'*, translated Richard Barry, Faber & Faber, London 1970.

Meissner, Otto: *Als Staatssekretär unter Ebert, Hindenburg und Hitler*, Hoffman & Campe, Hamburg 1950

Melnikow, Danil: *20 Juli 1944*, Deutsche Verlag der Wissenschaften, Berlin 1964

Michelet, Edmond: *Rue de la Liberté (Dachau)*, Editions du Seuil, Paris 1955

Misch, Carl: *Deutsche Geschichte im Zeitalter der Massen*, Kohlhammer Verlag, Stuttgart 1952

Moeller van den Bruck, Arthur: *Das dritte Reich*, Hanseatische Verlagsanstalt, Hamburg 1931

Mommsen, Hans: *Der Reichstagsbrand und seine politische Folgen, Vierteljahreshefte für Zeitgeschichte*, Stuttgart 1964

Münzenberg, Willy: *Propaganda als Waffe*, Editions du Carrefour, Paris 1937

Papen, Franz von: *Memoirs*, translated Brian Connell, André Deutsch, London 1952

Papen, Franz von: *Vom Scheitern einer Demokratie*, Hase & Koehler, Mainz 1968

Peis, Günter: *Naujocks, l'homme qui déclencha la guerre*, Arthaud, Paris 1962

Piotrowski, Stanislav: *Hans Frank's Diary*, Warsaw 1961

Rauschning, Hermann: *Hitler Speaks*, Thornton Butterworth, London 1940

Reed, Douglas: *The Burning of the Reichstag*, Victor Gollancz, London 1934

Reitlinger, Gerald: *The SS, Alibi of a Nation*, Wm. Heinemann, London, Melbourne & Toronto 1956

Reitlinger, G.: *The Final Solution*, Valentine Mitchell, London 1953

Remer, Otto: *20 Juli 1944*, Deutsche Opposition, Hamburg 1951

Ritter, Gerhard: *Carl Goerdeler und die deutsche Widerstandsbewegung*, Deutsche Verlagsanstalt, Stuttgart 1956

Röhm, Ernst: *Die Geschichte eines Hochverräters*, Franz Eher, Munich 1933

Rosenberg, Alfred: *Der Mythus des 20 Jahrhunderts*, Hoheneichen Verlag, Munich 1930

Rosenberg, Alfred: *Selected Writings*, edited by Robert Pois, Jonathan Cape, London 1970

BIBLIOGRAPHY

Rousset, David: *L'univers concentrationnaire*, Editions de Pavois, Paris 1946

Ruge, Wolfgang: *Die Deutsche Allgemeine Zeitung und die Brüning-Regierung*, Zeitschrift für Geschichtswissenschaft 1/1968, Berlin 1968

Schacht, Hjalmar: *Abrechnung mit Hitler*, Michaelis Verlag, Hamburg 1948

Schellenberg, Walter: *The Schellenberg Memoirs*, introduction Alan Bullock, translated Louis Hagen, André Deutsch, London 1961

Schlabrendorff, Fabian von: *The Secret War against Hitler*, translated Hilda Simon, Hodder & Stoughton, London 1961

Schlieffen, Alfred Graf von: *Cannae*, Berlin 1901

Schoenberner, Gerhard: *Wir haben es gesehen*, Hamburg 1962

Scholz, Arno: *Null Vier*, Arani Verlag, Berlin 1962

Schulze-Wilde, Harry: *Zur Geschichte der Technik der Nationalsozialistischen Machtergreifung*, Frankfurter Hefte 6/1957, Frankfurt 1957

Schuschnigg, Kurt von: *Austrian Requiem*, translated Franz von Hildebrand, Victor Gallancz, London 1947

Seeckt, General Hans von: *Aus meinem Leben*, Hase & Koehler, Leipzig 1940

Shirer, William L.: *The Rise and Fall of the Third Reich*, Secker & Warburg, London 1961

Skopin, W. I.: *Militarisme*, Moscow 1957

Speer, Albert: *Memoirs of Albert Speer*, translated Richard and Clara Winstone, Weidenfeld & Nicolson, London 1970

Spengler, Oswald: *The Hour of Decision*, translated Charles Atkinson, Allen & Unwin, London 1934

Stein, Adolf: *Gift, Feuer, Mord*, Brunnen Verlag, Berlin 1934

Steltzer, Theodor: *Sechzig Jahre Zeitgenosse*, List, Munich 1966

Stercken, Hans: *De Gaulle hat gesagt*, Nordwest-Verlag, Stuttgart 1967

Strasser, Otto: *Die deutsche Bartolomäusnacht*, Reso-Verlag, Zurich 1935

Strölin, Karl: *Stuttgart im Endstadium des Krieges*, Vorwerk, Stuttgart 1950

Thimme, Hans: *Weltkrieg ohne Waffen*, Cotta, Stuttgart and Berlin 1932

Thyssen, Fritz: *I paid Hitler*, Hodder & Stoughton, London 1941

Tippelskirch, Kurt von: *Geschichte des Zweiten Weltkrieges*, Athenäum Verlag, Bonn 1959

Treviranus, Gottfried Reinhold: *Das Ende von Weimar*, Econ Verlag, Düsseldorf 1968

Tobias, Fritz: *The Reichstag Fire*, translated Arnold Pomerans, Secker & Warburg, London 1963

Tobias, Fritz: *Das Geheimnis des Reichstagsbrandes*, Deutsche National-Zeitung und Soldaten-Zeitung, 1 March 1963

Toynbee, Arnold J. and V. M. (eds.): *Eve of the War, 1939*, Oxford University Press, London 1952

Trevor-Roper, Prof. H. R.: *The Last Days of Hitler*, Macmillan, London and New York 1956

Turner, Henry Ashby Jr.: 'Hitler's Secret Pamphlet for Industrialists', *Journal of Modern History*

Turner, Henry Ashby Jr.: 'Big Business and the Rise of Hitler', *American Historical Review*, October 1969

Wagner, Elizabeth: *Der Generalquartiermeister*, Olzog Verlag, Munich 1964

Warlimont, Walter: *Inside Hitler's Headquarters*, translated Richard H. Barry, Weidenfeld & Nicolson, London 1964

Weberstedt, Hans and Langner, Karl: *Gedenkhalle für die Gefallenen des Dritten Reiches*, Franz Eher, Munich 1935

Weinert, Erich: *Das Nationalkomitee 'Freies Deutschland'*, Rütten & Loening, Berlin 1957

Weisenborn, Günther: *Der lautlose Aufstand*, Rowohlt, Hamburg 1954

Weizsäcker, Ernst Freiherr von: *Erinnerungen*, Paul List Verlag, Munich, Leipzig and Freiburg 1950

Westphal, Siegfried: *The German Army in the West*, Cassell and Co., London 1951

Wiesenthal, Simon: *Doch die Mörder leben*, Munich 1967

Wulf, Josef: *Das Dritte Reich und seine Vollstrecker*, Arani Verlag, Berlin-Grünewald 1961

Zipfel, Friedrich: 'Krieg und Zusammenbruch' in *Das Dritte Reich*, Hefte zum Zeitgeschehen, Hannover 1961

Zipfel, Friedrich: *Terror und Widerstand*, Plötzensee, Berlin 1964

Zipfel, Friedrich: *Kirchenkampf in Deutschland*, Walter de Gruyter & Co., Berlin 1965

Zipfel, Friedrich: *Der Reichstagsbrand*, Villingen 1962

Zirpins, Walter: 'Das Getto von Litzmannstadt, kriminalpolizeilich gesehen' in *Kriminalistik* edited by Reinhard Heydrich, Sept./Oct. 1941

Zoller, A: *Hitler Privat*, Droste Verlag, Düsseldorf 1949

INDEX

INDEX